OPPOSING VIEWPOINTS® SERIES

Reproductive Technologies

Other Books of Related Interest:

Opposing Viewpoints Series
BioMedical Ethics

Cloning

Genetic Engineering

Current Controversies Series
Medical Ethics

At Issue Series
Creationism Versus Evolution

The Ethics of Genetic Engineering

The Ethics of Human Cloning

"Congress shall make no law ... abridging the freedom of speech, or of the press."

First Amendment to the U.S. Constitution

The basic foundation of our democracy is the First Amendment guarantee of freedom of expression. The Opposing Viewpoints Series is dedicated to the concept of this basic freedom and the idea that it is more important to practice it than to enshrine it.

OPPOSING VIEWPOINTS® SERIES

Reproductive Technologies

Clay Farris Naff, Book Editor

GREENHAVEN PRESS

An imprint of Thomson Gale, a part of The Thomson Corporation

Detroit • New York • San Francisco • New Haven, Conn. • Waterville, Maine • London

Christine Nasso, *Publisher*
Elizabeth Des Chenes, *Managing Editor*

For more information, contact:
Greenhaven Press
27500 Drake Rd.
Farmington Hills, MI 48331-3535
Or you can visit our Internet site at http://www.gale.com

LIBRARY OF CONGRESS CATALOGING-IN-PUBLICATION DATA

Reproductive technologies / Clay Farris Naff, book editor.
   p. cm. -- (Opposing viewpoints)
  Includes bibliographical references and index.
  ISBN-13: 978-0-7377-3331-0 (hardcover)
  ISBN-13: 978-0-7377-3332-7 (pbk.)
  1. Human reproductive technology--Juvenile literature. 2. Human reproductive technology--Moral and ethical aspects--Juvenile literature. I. Naff, Clay Farris.
  RG133.5.R475 2007
  618.1'7806--dc22
                                              2007004404

ISBN-10: 0-7377-3331-4 (hardcover)
ISBN-10: 0-7377-3332-2 (pbk.)

Printed in the United States of America
10 9 8 7 6 5 4 3 2 1

Contents

Chapter 3: Should Limits Be Placed on Current Reproductive Technologies?

Chapter 4: Should New Reproductive Technologies Be Pursued?

Why Consider Opposing Viewpoints?

> "The only way in which a human being can make some approach to knowing the whole of a subject is by hearing what can be said about it by persons of every variety of opinion and studying all modes in which it can be looked at by every character of mind. No wise man ever acquired his wisdom in any mode but this."
>
> *John Stuart Mill*

In our media-intensive culture it is not difficult to find differing opinions. Thousands of newspapers and magazines and dozens of radio and television talk shows resound with differing points of view. The difficulty lies in deciding which opinion to agree with and which "experts" seem the most credible. The more inundated we become with differing opinions and claims, the more essential it is to hone critical reading and thinking skills to evaluate these ideas. Opposing Viewpoints books address this problem directly by presenting stimulating debates that can be used to enhance and teach these skills. The varied opinions contained in each book examine many different aspects of a single issue. While examining these conveniently edited opposing views, readers can develop critical thinking skills such as the ability to compare and contrast authors' credibility, facts, argumentation styles, use of persuasive techniques, and other stylistic tools. In short, the Opposing Viewpoints series is an ideal way to attain the higher-level thinking and reading skills so essential in a culture of diverse and contradictory opinions.

In addition to providing a tool for critical thinking, Opposing Viewpoints books challenge readers to question their own strongly held opinions and assumptions. Most people form their opinions on the basis of upbringing, peer pressure, and personal, cultural, or professional bias. By reading carefully balanced opposing views, readers must directly confront new ideas as well as the opinions of those with whom they disagree. This is not to simplistically argue that everyone who reads opposing views will—or should—change his or her opinion. Instead, the series enhances readers' understanding of their own views by encouraging confrontation with opposing ideas. Careful examination of others' views can lead to the readers' understanding of the logical inconsistencies in their own opinions, perspective on why they hold an opinion, and the consideration of the possibility that their opinion requires further evaluation.

Evaluating Other Opinions

To ensure that this type of examination occurs, Opposing Viewpoints books present all types of opinions. Prominent spokespeople on different sides of each issue as well as well-known professionals from many disciplines challenge the reader. An additional goal of the series is to provide a forum for other, less known, or even unpopular viewpoints. The opinion of an ordinary person who has had to make the decision to cut off life support from a terminally ill relative, for example, may be just as valuable and provide just as much insight as a medical ethicist's professional opinion. The editors have two additional purposes in including these less-known views. One, the editors encourage readers to respect others' opinions—even when not enhanced by professional credibility. It is only by reading or listening to and objectively evaluating others' ideas that one can determine whether they are worthy of consideration. Two, the inclusion of such viewpoints encourages the important critical thinking skill of objectively evaluating an author's credentials and bias. This evaluation will illuminate an author's reasons for taking a particular stance on an issue and will aid in readers' evaluation of the author's ideas.

It is our hope that these books will give readers a deeper understanding of the issues debated and an appreciation of the complexity of even seemingly simple issues when good and honest people disagree. This awareness is particularly important in a democratic society such as ours in which people enter into public debate to determine the common good. Those with whom one disagrees should not be regarded as enemies but rather as people whose views deserve careful examination and may shed light on one's own.

Thomas Jefferson once said that "difference of opinion leads to inquiry, and inquiry to truth." Jefferson, a broadly educated man, argued that "if a nation expects to be ignorant and free . . . it expects what never was and never will be." As individuals and as a nation, it is imperative that we consider the opinions of others and examine them with skill and discernment. The Opposing Viewpoints series is intended to help readers achieve this goal.

David L. Bender and Bruno Leone,
Founders

Introduction

> *The blind conviction that we have to do something about other people's reproductive behavior, and that we may have to do it whether they like it or not, derives from the assumption that the world belongs to us . . . rather than to them . . . .*
>
> —Germaine Greer,
> feminist author

Every technology has its pros and cons, but reproductive technologies seem to present especially agonizing choices. For people suffering from infertility, the technologies offer the incomparable gift of a chance to have a child. For critics of the technologies, they variously present a threat to the well-being of children, to motherhood, to God's will, and to the future of humanity itself. These conflicting attitudes and passionate commitments appear to make a consensus nearly impossible to achieve.

However, societal experience of reproductive technologies suggests that the opportunities they offer will triumph over opposition, no matter how adamant that opposition may be. In short, reproductive technologies are here to stay.

The earliest intervention in reproduction—artificial insemination, introduced in the 1800s,—became entangled in the controversy over eugenics, the idea of improving humans through selective reproduction. Artificial insemination, write historians Cynthia R. Daniels and Janet Golden, "was a highly secretive medical procedure of questionable legal status in its early years. Only families deemed acceptable by doctors had access to this technology and it was up to physicians to find-the donors, who were typically selected for their physical resemblance to the husband and for their educational and professional attainments."

The idea that a successful father would donate his sperm to impregnate the wife of another man was shocking enough to nineteenth-century sensibilities, but adding to that a deliberate effort to raise intelligence or to increase physical fitness led to intense controversy. Eugenics got a bad name after the Nazis and many U.S. authorities applied it in explicitly racist ways. Nevertheless, while forced sterilization (one of the techniques of eugenics) has been banned, artificial insemination has survived and is now mainstream.

Similarly, the announcement of the birth of Louise Brown, the world's first "test-tube baby" conjured up visions of "the baby hatcheries in Aldous Huxley's *Brave New World*," as *Time* magazine aptly put it. The uproar soon died down, however, and now, despite the continuing opposition of the Catholic Church, in vitro fertilization, or IVF, has become commonplace. More than twenty-two hundred IVF clinics have sprung up worldwide, and more than two hundred thousand babies are born via the technology each year.

Of course, this does not guarantee that every innovation in reproductive technology will win acceptance. Surrogate mothering, in which a woman "rents" her womb to an infertile couple, is on the decline following a series of court battles over custody of the offspring.

An even more contentious issue is human reproductive cloning. Even before a viable technology had been developed, a host of laws were passed to prevent the creation of a baby who is the genetic twin of its only parent. Fifteen states presently have laws against human reproductive cloning on their books. Federal law prohibits funding research into such technologies.

Internationally, a number of countries, including the member states of the European Union, have also banned human cloning. In 2005 the United Nations weighed in with a declaration that calls on all member nations "to prohibit all forms of human cloning inasmuch as they are incompatible with human dignity and the protection of human life."

And yet, it is by no means certain that this web of laws guarantees that human cloning will not occur. Research into human cloning continues apace in many labs, in part because it holds a promise of curing many genetic diseases, providing tailor-made "spare parts," such as replacement retinas for people who have gone blind, and putting an end to widespread chronic maladies such as diabetes.

The scientists engaged in such research by and large have no interest in producing babies via cloning technology. They are focused on producing stem cells that have genes identical to the patient's but which can be coaxed into becoming any kind of organ.

Nevertheless, a few scientists and organizations claim to be vigorously pursuing human reproductive cloning—a few even claim to have succeeded, though no proof has been furnished. To some observers, this suggests that eventually human cloning will occur, and that once it does, public fears will subside and acceptance will follow. "By the time the first human clone becomes an adult," remarks Oxford philosopher Nick Bostrom, "the moral debates over cloning will probably be long forgotten."

Nevertheless, it remains uncertain whether human cloning will ever succeed. It may prove so unreliable a technology that no one would want to use it to have a baby. Some scientists are pessimistic: "It's just a big failure," Richard Schultz, a developmental and reproductive biologist at the University of Pennsylvania, told the *New York Times*. Animal cloning experiments to date have shown a high failure rate, and even when a successful birth is achieved, the clone often suffers from numerous health problems that scientists suspect are the result of cloning itself.

One way or the other, the issues surrounding human cloning will eventually be settled. That, however, will not mark the end of controversy in reproductive technologies. The business of fertility has grown enormously since the first successful IVF procedure in the 1970s. An estimated 12 percent of American couples experience fertility challenges, creating a domestic market of more than 7 million customers. In 2002, fertility clinics in the United States took in nearly $3 billion.

Competitive business pressures are already driving innovation. In recent years, for example, the IVF clinics have developed a procedure for injecting a man's sperm directly into an egg (rather than putting them both in a dish and waiting for nature to take its course). On the frontier of reproductive technology some scientists are experimenting with artificial wombs. Already, arguments are developing over whether this would be a beneficial technology or a monstrous threat to motherhood.

No one can forecast the future of technology, but one thing appears clear: despite religious and ethical objections, technological innovations that make life more convenient or pleasurable tend to be accepted over time. This is especially true in the area of reproduction, where contraceptives and abortion were once illegal and where every major innovation in fertility treatment has been greeted with howls of dismay. In *Opposing Viewpoints: Reproductive Technologies* the authors contribute various opinions and predictions regarding this fascinating debate in the following chapters: How Do Reproductive Technologies Impact Society? What Ethical Issues Arise in Reproductive Technologies? Should Limits Be Placed on Current Reproductive Technologies? and Should New Reproductive Technologies Be Pursued? Even if certain technologies fail or fade away, the trend toward more reproductive technologies in our lives appears to be irresistible.

OPPOSING
VIEWPOINTS®
SERIES

CHAPTER 1

How Do Reproductive Technologies Impact Society?

Chapter Preface

They say there are two sides to every issue. For many kinds of controversy, that is true. Gun control, in America at least, is an issue that falls neatly across political lines: those on the left tend overwhelmingly to support it, while those on the right tend overwhelmingly to oppose it. Opinions on reproductive technologies, by contrast, vary widely, with no consistent relation to political standpoint.

Many conservatives embrace fertility treatments, but many others consider them immoral. On the left, there are similar divisions among feminists: some are adamantly opposed to reproductive technologies, while others embrace them as a path to reproductive liberation.

Faith plays a large role in how people view reproductive technologies, but again it does not produce consistent results. The Catholic hierarchy is strictly opposed to any artificial intervention in the reproductive process, whether to promote pregnancy or prevent it. It should be noted, however, that a substantial number of American Catholic couples defy the church's teaching in this area. Evangelical Christians, on the whole, have welcomed fertility treatments as furthering the Bible's injunction to be fruitful and multiply. Muslims generally accept fertility treatments on similar grounds, except when they involve donated sperm or eggs, which are considered forbidden by Islam.

All such perspectives color the opinions of people as to whether reproductive technologies are helpful or hurtful to couples, their offspring, and society as a whole. To some critics, the risks that egg donation, surrogacy, and other procedures present to women should categorize reproductive technologies as harmful. To others, the chance to overcome infertility and join the ranks of parenthood makes the risk trivial compared to the payoff. To still others, the risk that children born through reproductive technologies will suffer physical or psychological harm is not acceptable. Finally, there are those who view the rise of reproductive technologies as heralding the demise of traditional families and the dawn of a bizarre new social order. For them, reproductive technologies are clearly a grave development. Yet, just as clearly, the vast majority of those who successfully participate in reproductive technologies, either as donors or recipients, find deep satisfaction in the results. In the pages that follow, readers will be able to see for themselves the breadth and scope of these many viewpoints.

"Why does anyone, religious or not, think that forming artificial families is acceptable?"

Reproductive Technologies Destroy Families

Tricia Smith Vaughan

In the following selection Tricia Smith Vaughan calls for a broad rejection of what she terms "artificial families." She notes that even traditional adoption deprives a baby of its mother's milk. She blames mental health professionals for redefining family, thereby opening the door to artificial reproductive technologies that threaten the future of natural motherhood. She charges that in vitro fertilization, surrogate motherhood, and similar technologies will desensitize people to the point where mothers may entirely disappear. Tricia Smith Vaughan is a mother of three who performs comedy as "The Comic Mom" in various venues and writes a column for News with Views, *as well as for other publications. Before she became a mom, she taught first-year English composition and literature for five years at North Carolina State University in Raleigh.*

Tricia Smith Vaughan, "No More Mommies?" September 30, 2005. www.NewsWith Views.com. Reproduced by permission.

As you read, consider the following questions:

1. Why does Vaughan think American couples who adopt Asian babies are being cruel?
2. What personal experience may have contributed to the author's views?
3. What specific potential technological development does Vaughan fear could put an end to natural mothering?

Many Christians oppose the idea of two women or two men forming a supposed family by taking someone else's children or paying someone to incubate a child or being impregnated with some anonymous father's sperm. I don't know why the religious only seem concerned when this family tampering occurs with homosexuals. Why does anyone, religious or not, think that forming artificial families is acceptable?

Most churchgoers congratulate a husband and wife who've just returned from China, complete with Asian baby girl in tow, an infant cut off from her family and culture. The Asian mother and extended family, subjected to a horrendous system that forces parents to abandon their baby girls, are hardly given a second thought. Nor do those who congratulate seem to consider the cruelty of forcing the traumatized baby into an extreme and permanent culture change.

Similarly, when people who've used someone else's egg or sperm to conceive hire a surrogate to carry a baby, or have a doctor's help in creating five or six embryos, only to use two or three, others congratulate them as well, not realizing the effect that unnaturally conceiving children has on the life of the surrogate whose womb is used or on the life of the human being that this method creates.

Mother's Milk

Many adoption agencies allude to Moses as the first adoptee, creating the illusion that adoption itself has somehow been sanctioned by God. What adoption agencies leave out of Moses' story is that the Egyptian king at the time was commanding midwives to kill every male child. Yes, midwives. When the midwives obeyed God and refused the king's order, the king asked the people to "cast into the Nile" every Hebrew male child. Moses' mother tried to save her son's life by hiding him as long as she could. When a girl found him in the bulrushes, the girl "went and called the child's mother" to nurse baby Moses. (Exodus 1:15–22, 2:8)

Let's compare that to the current adoption scene. Rather than calling on the mother to ensure that the baby has the best possible food, women who adopt either pump their body full of hormones so that they can pretend to breastfeed or feed the baby artificial formula, even when they know who and where the child's mother is. Men have even undergone this bizarre scheme, pretending to nurse a baby. Breastfeeding by a baby's true mother is so natural and helpful to the child that I can't help but wonder why babies are whisked away, often immediately after birth, and the mother is discarded like last month's magazines. Moses' mother, however, remained important to Moses.

When Moses was an adult, he "went out to his people and looked on their burdens." (Exodus 2:11) Note that the people referred to here are the Hebrews, not the Egyptians who raised him. Imagine this scenario in today's adoption world, in which most states seal truthful birth records and falsify the birth certificates that we adoptees must use. When my own natural mother, from whom I was separated for over 34 years, called the Office of Vital Records in the state in which I was born, she was told that she could not obtain my birth certificate; the worker's exact words were "it's as if you never had a child." Does anyone believe that God wants mothers to be treated this way?

Natural Parents Are Irreplaceable

And yet, most people will go right along with taking a child from its mother. They congratulate the taker and pretend—right along with the $1.5 billion U.S. adoption industry—that the child has miraculously acquired a new set of parents, falsified birth certificate and all. The truth is that while we have many people who may function in a parental role in our life, we all only have one set of true parents, one mommy and one daddy. Sometimes we are separated, physically, legally, emotionally, or a combination of these, from those parents. Parents, however people like to deny it, can never be replaced. Only when we realize that every child has only one mom and one dad will the idea of "two mommies" become the absurdity that it should be.

Recycling children via adoption has not always been so popular: Prior to 1900, "the general trend . . . seemed to be to attempt to keep mother and child together." . . . With so many benefits, emotionally and physically, for the breastfeeding child, this arrangement still seems to be the one that is truly in the best interest of the child. . . .

"Parent" Is Not a Verb

Unfortunately for the family, the definition of parent and family has fallen under the whims of the mental health professionals. Social workers and media eager to help them began so successfully deeming people parents who weren't that we began, in the latter part of the twentieth century, to refer to "parent" as a verb, as if everyday I wake up and decide whether or not I'll be parenting my children today. In reality, parenting is done at conception. It is a transitory state of fatherhood and motherhood that the media have promoted to us that has helped to weaken our family structure. The truth is more lasting: Parents are created at natural conception and do not change throughout a child's life.

In our brave new society, we refuse to believe such permanence. Parents are interchangeable; children are recyclable. If God does not bless us with a child, we cheat. We covet and take someone else's eggs or their child or we sidestep God and go to a fertility doctor who can help us concoct the family we want, selecting for sex or other characteristics if we like. Children are no longer looked upon as a blessing, but as a right. If we are not blessed with any, we believe that we have every right to obtain one, by any means possible.

With such an atmosphere, it's easy to see how natural parents began losing their value. My own father was not allowed to communicate with my mother while she was locked in her maternity home prison. It's hard to be a good dad when you're never allowed to see your child. But separation of the family, including allowing the father to wash his hands completely of the whole situation, and not listing him on the true birth certificate, was part of the plan. Having a father interfere with social workers' supposed counseling of the mother by proposing marriage or talking with the mother would slow the supply of babies. According to Nathan Cohen's *Social Work and Social Problems*, published in 1964, the demand for babies in my year of birth was already growing:

> "Because there are many more married couples wanting to adopt newborn white babies than there are babies, it may almost be said that they, rather than out of wedlock babies, are a social problem. (Sometimes social workers in adoption agencies have facetiously suggested setting up social provisions for more 'baby breeding.')"

Excess Demand for Babies

Add single people and homosexuals to the list and you've got an even higher demand for babies today. Babies are being imported from China, Russia, Guatamala, and other countries to fill the demand. Never fear, however, there's a new idea that will help increase the supply of babies. Studies show that

The End of Mommy and Daddy?

In Spain, all birth certificates have been changed from listing "Mother" and "Father" to "Progenitor A" and "Progenitor B."

The old classic "Daddy's Little Girl" now becomes, "You're the end of the rainbow, my pot of gold, you're Progenitor B's little girl to have and hold."

Earlier [in 2007], the Commonwealth of Virginia issued a birth certificate to an adoptive couple that read Parent 1 and Parent 2.

Canadians have erased the term "natural parent" and replaced it with "legal parent."

The roles once determined by a man, a woman and a pregnancy are now increasingly determined by the state.

The Commission on Parenthood's Future, a nonpartisan group of scholars and leaders concerned with marriage, family, law and culture, recently released a white paper titled "The Revolution in Parenthood." The revolution is that the "two-person, mother-father model of parenthood is being fundamentally challenged."

Lori Borgman, Salon, January 2, 2007.

separation from our mother, even at birth, can have devastating effects on children. Soon, however, we may find that mothers are completely discarded. I first learned about artificial wombs when I read an article about them a couple of years ago. Now, we learn that artificial wombs are a mere twenty years away. These artificial wombs "would both expand the range of reproductive choices and make the differences between men and women matters of technological convention rather than biological nature." Well, we wouldn't want biological nature to interfere with technology, would we?

Threat to Motherhood

With formula feeding, we manage to separate children from their mother after birth. With stranger adoption, we take children from their natural families and place them with families that aren't their own, asking everyone to pretend that these children belong in those families. With embryo adoption, we separate children from their mother before birth, giving the woman who carries the child the extra benefit of being able to tell the child about the pregnancy. Is it any wonder that mothers ourselves and our most important function of giving birth may soon be deemed obsolete? Could it be that one day, potential moms may be asking, "Why take the risk of gestating my child in an old-fashioned womb?"

The next time you become angry at a couple who claims to be "two mommies," ask yourself how often you've capitulated to the rhetoric of this brave new world, how often you've called someone who's never given birth and passed along genes a mother, or how often you've looked at an Asian child with two people who are clearly not her parents and believed that they are family. And then remember this scene from Aldous Huxley's *Brave New World*, describing a world in which babies are decanted, according to society's demands:

> When questioned about the word "parent," "there was an uneasy silence. Several of the boys blushed" at what they had learned was smut. The Hatchery Director helps them out: "The parents were the father and the mother," the director explained to the young boys, who had learned that family was as derogatory as any four-letter word our present-day mind can think of. 'Mother,' [the director] "repeatedly loudly ... leaning back in his chair, 'These,' he said gravely, 'are unpleasant facts; I know it. But then most historical facts are unpleasant.'"

In Huxley's book, babies are decanted in a hatchery, not born to a mother. Mothers and fathers are part of an ugly past and embryos are conditioned to be in a certain caste for

27

life. Mothers are not only unnecessary but looked upon as smut. Family is a dirty word. In the past half-century, we have been encouraging mothers to give their child away and we call the people who take the child "parents," when "guardian" would be an honest term.

Loss of Perspective

With the advent of in-vitro fertilization and other reproductive technologies, many women often think that they have every right to have a child, whatever the means. If the technologies don't work, then people pay someone else to carry a child, asking another woman to give away the baby who's been attached to her for nine months. Some take a mother's child, rationalizing how much better off the child would be with them rather than its true parents.

These methods of cheating desensitize us, making it easier for us to say that a child can have two mommies; in a few years, we'll be saying that a child can have no mother. In fact, Michael Jackson has already claimed that about his own supposed children, on nationwide television. As we head toward this brave new world, let us not blame only homosexual activists for leading us away from true family. The people who approved of stranger adoption and who sat silently while fertility doctors performed their hocus pocus to create babies in a test tube are now reaping what has been sown. When mothers cease to exist, we will have only ourselves to blame.

"[Reproductive technologies help] individuals experiencing infertility in their goal to build healthy families."

Reproductive Technologies Help Families

Bonnie Gilbert

Reproduction is a major stage in life, notes Bonnie Gilbert in the following selection taken from her letter to the President's Council on Bioethics, and infertility is the disease that stands in its way. More than six million couples in the United States suffer from infertility. Reproductive technologies help them overcome the problem. The technologies and procedures that help couples overcome infertility need to be regulated, she concedes, but adds that such regulation should be balanced with the need to provide access to reproductive technologies to infertile couples. Also, the government should respect the privacy and autonomy of patients seeking fertility treatments, she argues. The current system, Gilbert claims, is working relatively well and should be left alone so that individuals can continue to make decisions about fertility treatments for themselves. At the time of writing, Bonnie Gilbert was acting executive director of RESOLVE, a nonprofit organization that promotes equal access to family-building options for people experiencing infertility.

Bonnie Gilbert, "Letter to the General Counsel of the President's Council on Bioethics," RESOLVE, April 2003. www.resolve.org. Reproduced by permission.

As you read, consider the following questions:

1. According to Gilbert, what proportion of American couples of reproductive age suffers from infertility?

2. When it comes to decision making, what sets fertility patients apart from other medical populations, in the author's opinion?

3. What step does Gilbert say RESOLVE endorses to increase access to fertility treatments?

Infertility is a disease or condition that results in the abnormal functioning of the male or female reproductive system, which interferes with the ability of a man or woman to achieve a pregnancy or of a woman to carry a pregnancy to live birth. Both the American Society for Reproductive Medicine (ASRM) and the American College of Obstetricians and Gynecologists (ACOG) recognize infertility as a disease. The United States Supreme Court has ruled that reproduction is a major life activity under the Americans with Disabilities Act. This ruling demonstrates the importance of reproduction and the impact that infertility has on the lives of men and women and on society at large.

Common Affliction

According to the National Center for Health Statistics, infertility affects 6.1 million people in the United States. This figure represents 1 in 10 couples in which the woman is of reproductive age—this very significant number demonstrates that infertility affects a huge percentage of our population. That impact, of course, is an immediate and direct one on the sufferers of the disease. Couples in their most active and productive years are distracted by the physical and emotional hardships of the disease. Infertility is a crisis of the body, a crisis of the mind and a crisis of the spirit and calls into question a person's view of themselves, his or her life goals, his or her faith, his or her relationship with their spouse, and others. Infertility impacts a couple's general health, their marriage, job performance and social interactions—it brings a deep sense of grief and loss. Infertility also exacts an enormous toll on society. The social norm in the United States is one that heavily encourages, if not expects, married couples to bear and raise children, and questions the values of couples who do not.

Infertility treatment is an important aspect of reproductive health care. There is a growing recognition among consumer and medical groups that infertility treatment should be included as part of a basic medical benefits package. According to a November 1999 poll, conducted by Peter Hart Research, the majority of Americans believe health care coverage should include costs associated with infertility treatment.

RESOLVE supports the rights of individuals experiencing infertility in their goal to build healthy families and to protect their options in those family-building goals. RESOLVE supports the right of individuals to elect their family-building method(s), including appropriate medical treatment, such as, but not limited to, ART [assisted reproductive technology], adoption, and third-party agreements. RESOLVE works to ensure access to appropriate medical treatments for all who are impacted by the disease, and supports the goal of the patient in expecting a safe outcome of those procedures for mothers and their future children. RESOLVE supports the right of those with infertility to make private decisions regarding their medical treatment with the assistance of qualified, board-certified physicians. RESOLVE supports and defends the right of individuals to be free from interference in making the very personal decision about the uses of their own body tissues, including reproductive tissues and fertilized reproductive tissues.

Regulation Assures Excellence

As has been established, infertility is a disease. However, we recognize that this disease is unique even within the realm of reproductive diseases. Because of that, we understand that this committee is questioning the current regulatory environment of the treatment of infertility. RESOLVE firmly believes the current regulatory environment for assisted reproduction, embryo research and human genetics works phenomenally well, and is a testament to the demands that infertile patients have required for safe and effective treatment, the dedication of the medical profession in providing the safest, most efficacious treatment possible and the profession's ongoing and continued commitment to investigating better treatment protocols.... The Fertility Clinic Success Rate and Certification Act of 1992 requires clinics that practice assisted reproductive technology to supply data on their success rates, and that that data be published by the CDC [Centers for Disease Control and Prevention]. The profession and industry are subject also to the Clinical Laboratories and Improvement Act requirements of quality control, and the reproductive professionals have adopted quite rigorous practice guidelines to ensure safety and efficacy. Various government agencies, the FDA [Food and Drug Administration] and others, have also made clear their authority to regulate certain aspects of these technologies. Additionally, NCOART—the National Coalition for Oversight of Assisted Reproductive Technologies is a voluntary group consisting of patient advocacy groups including RESOLVE, ASRM, SART [Society for Assisted Reproductive Technology], FDA, NIH [National Institutes of Health], ABA [American Bar Association] reproductive law section, CDC, and AATB [American Association of Tissue Banks], that meets to discuss issues to ART. Does this mean that there are areas within the laws that govern these regulations that cannot be improved upon? Of course not.

But the current regulatory environment of these technologies provides to infertility patients and their prospective offspring an extremely safe and high-quality level of medical care. In addition, our system is one in which ample information is readily available to infertility patients as to the success rates of various clinics and to the certification of providers. We know of no other patient population that has such a wealth of information available to them. In fact, the reason for the existence of RESOLVE is to provide infertility patients with a wealth of information about treatment options, and in turn, the patients demand a high level of information from their doctors about the risks and benefits of any given protocol and the alternatives to such treatment. We know firsthand that infertility patients take their medical care even more serious than patients of any other disease groups. Why? Because they recognize that their decisions about medical care will have a direct impact on someone beyond their own self—their offspring. We can assure you that this population of prospective parents evaluates what is in the best interest of their children far more diligently than the general population. Infertility patients are a well-informed group, who make careful and deliberate decisions about their care, who question in minute detail every single contingency associated with treatment and weigh carefully the risks and benefits of each contingency, and who at the same time weigh alternative options for family building.

RESOLVE was established to help patients with this very deliberate decision-making process. RESOLVE offers a "Questions to Ask" series that aids patients in their communications with medical professionals, which encourages patients to ask detailed, probing and informed questions of their doctors. RESOLVE keeps a physician referral list of qualified medical professionals that patients can access, a list which provides great detail about the areas of expertise of physicians and only board-certified physicians are listed. RESOLVE offers its members a network of patients who can provide their own personal experiences regarding a variety of treatment options. RESOLVE provides its members a variety of forums, a member-to-member referral system, an on-staff medical expert, a HelpLine staffed by individuals who have undergone treatment, an online bulletin board, local support group meetings, all of which aid the individual in the process that is required to become an informed infertility patient necessary to make important family-building decisions.

Patients' Rights Are Crucial

RESOLVE's primary concern, however, is that the regulation of biotechnologies used to treat the disease of infertility must be balanced with the very important priority of access to treatment, safety of the treatment and patient privacy. We are concerned about heavy regulation of clinical practice for several reasons. First and foremost, heavy regulation by government is likely to remove or restrict reproductive decisions from the place where decisions should lie—with the individual patient. We will advocate against attempts to restrict this vital individual freedom. There is no other disease group in which the care is regulated as heavily as the care provided today to infertile patients. We are also concerned that regulation would be financed by patients and not properly funded in a health care system like the one the U.S. currently employs.

We must take this opportunity to say a few words about the U.S. health care delivery system. Rationing of services, or the decision to deliver less than the optimum level of effective health care due to levels of priorities amongst the competing demands on the health care system, pervades all systems of health care delivery, including the U.S. health care delivery system. Infertility is one of those diseases that falls into the category of extreme forms of rationing—denial of services or exclusion of those services to portions of the population because it is not a reimbursable health service under the health care menu of most employee benefit or insurance plans. RESOLVE endorses state and federal legislation that will require insurers to cover the costs of appropriate treatment because it would result in greater access to the treatments for a greater

Ignorance Masks Infertility Crisis

"It is shocking to see, in this day and age with 1 in 8 couples of childbearing age in this country battling infertility and more media coverage than ever on reproductive health issues, that so few Americans are aware of how prevalent the disease is in our society.... While much of this can be attributed to the stigma still assigned to infertility, a lot of responsibility lies in the way in which we, as a society, fear talking about or being associated with the disease."

Joseph Isaacs, RESOLVE, 2005.
www.resolve.org.

number of the population (and all those who need the treatment). Decisions that are made during an ART procedure must be strictly medical decisions, not financial ones.

The characteristics of the health care delivery system matter when attempts are made to ration or regulate services. What works in England—a system of social insurance—will not work in the U.S.—a unique system that, we can all agree, is very complicated in its design. For example, a policy that requires a firm limit on the number of embryos transferred during an ART procedure is unworkable in our health care delivery system. It injects the government into a decision-making process that is a medical one, a process that the doctor providing the services and the patient must make in concert together based upon the medical needs of the patient and the appropriate medical treatment for that patient, just like for other diseases.

Infertility patients already recognize that they are financing out of pocket all research into infertility and that nearly 100 percent of infertility research is occurring in the private, for-profit environment. We support increased funding for key government agencies to ensure the security of the biotechnology industry's investment in research and development and the safety of treatment for patients. But we firmly believe that Americans, who need treatment today, because the success of treatment depends heavily on the age of the patient, will be denied that treatment in a heavily regulated system. As has been the history of most U.S. government regulatory bodies, the body employs a lengthy and difficult review process of any treatment protocol and is funded by budgets that are subject to an annual appropriation from Congress. The length of the regulatory process and the uncertainty of congressional budgets would thus further deny patient care. Our model of health care delivery, coupled with the U.S. structure of government, complicates any thoughtful discussion about regulation of these types of biotechnologies.

Regulation of Embryo Research

RESOLVE believes that while human embryos at any stage are worthy of special respect and consideration, most of them will never be capable of giving rise to a baby. Stem cells are derived from human embryos developed for in-vitro fertilization that are in excess of the infertile couple's need. If these excess cells are not used for research or offered to other infertile couples (both are ethical options) they will be discarded. Nearly half of infertile couples say they would like to see some good come from their biological tissue that would otherwise become medical waste and feel that use of these cells in research to help save lives is extremely important. That is why RESOLVE is involved in the current debate about stem cell research and cloning.

Embryonic stem cells hold tremendous promise and could provide the missing link needed to cure some of the world's most deadly diseases. Up to 100 million Americans may benefit from this research and the suffering of millions could end. We believe it is immoral to impede research that could possibly cure the disease of a person living and breathing, but suffering today. While it is doubtful there would be an immediate benefit from this type of research into cures for those touched by infertility, our support of stem cell research and somatic cell nuclear transfer technology for therapeutic cloning purposes provides us with opportunities for dialogue with lawmakers who are part of the larger public policy debate about the future of biomedical research. Equally important, RESOLVE opposes any effort that would allow reproductive cloning, a technique we believe, at this time, is unsafe, irresponsible and unethical.

RESOLVE's position on stem cell research and cloning does not mandate the destruction of embryos. Again, we know that most embryos will not become a life. We would like to reiterate that infertility patients should be free from interference in making the very personal decision about the uses of their own body tissues, including reproductive tissues and fertilized reproductive tissues.

Patients Care Most About Safety

RESOLVE's first and last priority is the safety of the medical treatment available to infertile individuals. What infertility patients lack in financing their treatments, they make up for in education about their treatment. Like all prospective parents, infertility patients have as their foremost concern the safety of their future children and carefully consider that the actions they take on a daily basis can determine the quality of health, well being and life experience of their offspring. We would argue that these patients make the decision to procreate with even more careful thought and examination than those in the general public. In fact, it is at the far end of the "deliberate and careful" spectrum where these decisions are being made.

The ASRM guidelines for informed consent process employed by clinics is recommended to provide a written document which describes for patients the treatment protocol, including the efficacy and the risks not only to the patient, but also the possible risk to the subsequent child as well as alternative procedures and non-medical therapies for building a family.

No More Regulation Required

As with any other disease, Americans diagnosed with infertility have a right to privacy in deciding—working with medical professionals—the course of treatment they wish to pursue. This is not an area in which government agencies should be interfering, especially when there are no major flaws in the current system and when government budgets are strained.

The bottom line is that sufferers of infertility desire to fulfill a fundamental aspect of life—the desire to bear children and raise a family. And just like any couple making the very important decision to procreate, infertility patients weigh very carefully, how their own health (physical and mental), health history, family health history, lifestyle, and life experiences will affect the life of their offspring. We would argue that infertility patients make this decision with even more careful thought and examination than the population at large. Attempts to heavily regulate the treatments used to help couples build their families, as has been done in countries with a health care delivery system quite different from ours, will prove unworkable in the U.S. health care delivery system. Policymakers need to recognize that the characteristics of the system of government play an important role. RESOLVE urges caution in consideration of policies that will slow reproductive technologies and policies that are rigid by design. We will be diligent in our work to protect the rights of individuals to make private decisions about family building.

*"The substantial risks to egg donors are
not offset by any clear benefit."*

Egg Donation Puts
Women at Risk

Judy Norsigian

Demand for egg donations from women has been growing rapidly. They are used both for fertility treatments and for research. To meet this demand doctors typically extract multiple eggs from a single donor. According to the author of the following viewpoint, Judy Norsigian, this practice puts women's health at risk. The drugs that are used to hyperstimulate a donor's ovaries may cause a wide range of symptoms, including a pounding heart, sleeplessness, and pain, she argues. Norsigian is best known as coauthor of the book Our Bodies, Ourselves. *She cofounded the Boston Women's Health Book Collective and serves as the organization's executive director.*

As you read, consider the following questions:

1. What new technique is adding to the demand for egg donation, according to Norsigian?
2. What does the author say women should know about the FDA's approval of the drug Lupron?

Judy Norsigian, "Egg Donation Dangers," *GeneWatch*, September-October 2005. www.gene-watch.org. Reproduced with permission of *GeneWatch*, printed by the Council for Responsible Genetics.

3. Why is multiple egg extraction the norm, according to Norsigian?

Because embryonic stem cell research is poised to expand greatly, and somatic cell nuclear transfer (SCNT), a cloning technique in which the nucleus of an unfertilized egg is replaced with the nucleus from a body cell, requires large numbers of women to donate eggs for research purposes, there is renewed attention to the larger question of risks to women's health from egg extraction procedures. Whether eggs are extracted for reproductive purposes—as is the case in an infertility clinic where women undergo in vitro fertilization (IVF)—or for research purposes like SCNT, the risks involved in the procedure are the same.

Because SCNT is such a rapidly growing field of research, the demand for eggs is growing as well. Since women normally produce a single egg in their monthly menstrual cycles, and the number of donors is relatively low, embryo researchers attempt to stimulate donors' ovaries to produce a larger number of eggs. Gonadotropin hormone [which stimulates reproductive function] regimens are administered, and although fertility doctors try not to over-stimulate their patients' ovaries, complications can and do occur.

Risky Drugs

The risks of multiple egg extraction do not only come in this stage of the process, however. Lupron, or leuprolide acetate, is a drug that is commonly used to shut down a woman's ovaries before stimulating them to produce multiple follicles. This drug has caused a range of problems, according to the Food and Drug Administration (FDA). Theses include rashes, vasodilation (dilation of blood vessels causing a "hot flash"), burning sensations, tingling, itching, headaches and migraines, dizziness, hives, hair loss, severe non-inflammatory joint pain, difficulty breathing, chest pain, nausea, depression, emotional instability, loss of libido, dimness of vision, fainting, weakness, asthenia gravis hypophyseogenea (severe weakness due to loss of pituitary function), amnesia, hypertension, rapid heart rate, muscular pain, bone pain, abdominal pain, insomnia, swelling of hands, general edema, chronic enlargement of the thyroid, liver function abnormality, anxiety, and vertigo. Although the FDA approved the drug for several specific uses, such as the treatment of endometriosis and fibroid-associated anemia, it has not approved Lupron for use in multiple egg extraction procedures—something that is not well understood by many women who undergo these procedures. It is legal to use a drug for a non-approved use such as this, as long as it is marketed legally for at least one approved use. Lupron is just one of many drugs used "off-label" in this fashion. However, proper studies justifying its use for egg extraction have never been formally submitted to the FDA.

Severe Side Effects

The drugs used to hyperstimulate the ovaries also have negative effects, most notably a condition called Ovarian Hyperstimulation Syndrome (OHSS). Serious cases of this syndrome involve the development of cysts and enlargement of the ovaries, along with massive fluid build-up in the body. As noted in an article in *Human Reproduction Update*, "the reported prevalence of the severe form of OHSS is small, ranging from .05% to 5% [of women undergoing gonadotropin regimens]. Nevertheless, as this is an iatrogenic [medically induced] complication of a non-vital treatment with a potentially fatal outcome, the syndrome remains a serious problem for specialists dealing with infertility."

Also, as noted by Dr. Suzanne Parisian, a former Chief Medical Officer at the FDA, "OHSS carries an increased risk of clotting disorders, kidney damage, and ovarian twisting. Ovarian stimulation in general has been associated with serious life threatening pulmonary conditions in FDA trials including thromboembolic events, pulmonary embolism, pulmonary infarction, cerebral vascular accident (stroke) and arterial occlusion with loss of a limb and death." One Institutional Review Board (IRB) for Advanced Cell Technology in Massachusetts cited the risks as including "high blood pressure; fluid accumulation in the limbs; formation of blood clots which potentially could be dislodged from the involved vein or artery causing damage to vital organs such as lungs, heart or brain; intestinal problems such as decreased appetite, constipation; nausea and vomiting, diarrhea, difficulty in swallowing; intestinal bleeding, intestinal ulcers and polyps; thyroid enlargement; breast tenderness; hot flashes; bone, muscle and joint pain; anxiety; depression; blurred vision; mood swings; nervousness; numbness; taste changes; memory problems; lightheadedness; blackouts; and headaches."

Better to Protect Women

So why is multiple egg extraction the norm in IVF clinics? With such risks involved, why don't specialists just extract the single egg that women normally release each month? The obvious reason is that if only one egg is harvested using the natural cycling that occurs each month in most women, there is a good possibility that it will not be successfully fertilized. If fertilized, it may not develop into an embryo that could be successfully implanted into a woman's uterus, thus requiring repeated surgical procedures to extract more eggs. With each IVF procedure, extracting multiple eggs obviously increases the likelihood of success.

The same reasoning can be applied to the research context, as it is important to have a larger number of eggs with which to conduct research. But, given the early stages of embryo stem cell research, with only hypothetical benefits at hand, it may be far wiser to protect women from the risks of multiple egg extraction solely for SCNT research purposes and to permit only surgical extraction of the usually single egg

© CartoonStock.com

produced each month. Others argue that whatever the risks are—known and unknown—a woman should nevertheless have the choice to take these risks, especially if she has a strong personal investment in seeing certain therapies developed, even if they are only a distant promise.

Those who oversee the ethical conduct of research, especially members of IRBs, are supposed to think carefully about risk/benefit ratios when deciding whether to approve a research protocol. Embryo cloning research poses significant challenges in this regard. The aforementioned IRB approved a protocol for SCNT several years ago and included in the informed consent document the following language: "Severe lung and blood clot events have resulted in death." They clearly decided that it was ethical to ask women to take such risks as long as they informed them about them. Others might argue just the opposite.

Too Little Data

Reading the stories of young women who agreed to be multiple egg donors for IVF clinics and ended up with tragic consequences give reason to think carefully about whether these risks are justifiable in the research context. Many advocates believe that such risk-taking would not be ethical, partly because true informed consent is not possible in the absence of better data, particularly regarding Lupron.

One of the more serious issues needing far greater attention is the absence of quality long-term safety data on the infertility drugs commonly used. There are hundreds, if not thousands, of anecdotal reports, however, showing that complications are not short-lived. As noted in a three-part series in the *Boston Herald*:

> Seven of the women interviewed for this story say they suffered memory loss and bone aches while on Lupron, and that the problems continue years after stopping the drug. Some say seizures and serious vision problems that started while on Lupron also haven't gone away.
>
> One woman, Linda Abend in southern New Jersey, started a National Lupron Victims Network after her 34-year-old sister was hospitalized with seizures while taking Lupron in 1991 for a benign fibroid. Abend says her sister continues to suffer daily seizures, plus debilitating bone and muscle pain eight years later. And Abend said she has heard from more than 1,000 people nationwide—mostly women—who also report serious side effects that continue after stopping Lupron.
>
> The FDA says it has not tracked claims of such long-term effects. . . .

In a report submitted by TAP Pharmaceuticals to the FDA in April 1998, researchers wrote that they were "concerned" because more than one-third of the women they studied who took Lupron did not "demonstrate either partial reversibility" or "a trend toward return"' of bone mass in the six months after they stopped taking the drug. Further, the researchers noted some women lost as much as 7.3 percent of their bone density during treatment—more than twice the amount the drug's packaging lists in its warnings. The researchers concluded, "A more complete assessment of the effects of Lupron on [bone density] can only be made with longer term follow-up of these patients."

Questionable Benefit

Some women's health advocates argue that it is premature to collect eggs for SCNT, especially when it involves multiple egg extraction, because the substantial risks to egg donors are not offset by any clear benefit. In the case of IVF, the best infertility clinics can now offer 30–40% success rates, so that women undergoing multiple egg extraction—whether to achieve a pregnancy themselves, or to be an egg donor for another woman—know that there is a clear potential benefit, and one that is of inestimable value: a baby.

The risk/benefit ratio is vastly different in the case of SCNT, where the possible benefits of such research at this stage are entirely hypothetical. It is far from clear that SCNT will lead to any viable therapies, and much of what we need to know can be learned from studying embryo stem cells derived from embryos that would otherwise be discarded by couples who are no longer pursuing IVF. Thousands of such embryos are now available at infertility clinics and could be used for embryo stem cell research. When embryo stem cell research begins to offer possible therapies, perhaps a stronger case can then be made for pursuing SCNT.

Although SCNT is likely to provide an opportunity to study the progression of certain rare diseases, some of this research can be pursued with embryos, rejected during the increasing prevalent process of preimplantation genetic diagnosis (PGD). These, too, are embryos that would not be used for reproduction, and thus would be discarded unless they were used for research.

Caution Is Called For

Given that, even with new, more efficient techniques, researchers in South Korea needed to extract 185 eggs before they were able to produce a single cloned embryo, from which they could develop a line of embryonic stem cells to study further, pressure will increase to accelerate the collection of eggs through more widespread use of multiple egg extraction. Already, advertisements for egg donors are commonplace on many college campuses, where young women are motivated to undergo egg extractions for much-needed income, $4,000–7,000 per extraction in most cases, as well as for altruistic reasons. Both of these motivations could influence thousands more young and/or economically disadvantaged women to undergo risky egg extraction procedures solely for research, under circumstances where the risk/benefit ratio is far less clear. Once again, this will be an arena where we will see the mantra of "reproductive choice" co-opted and falsely applied.

In addition, new techniques may be developed that would obviate the need to use hormones for multiple egg extraction, providing even more justification for a cautious approach. A technique called "in vitro maturation," or IVM, may make it possible to obtain multiple eggs without hormone injections. An article in the July 15, 2003 *New York Times* claims, "Doctors have found that a few days before ovulation, as many as 30 to 50 egg follicles have begun to mature. Normally, only one will fully ripen for ovulation, and the rest are lost. But if the eggs are removed before ovulation, many of them can be matured in the laboratory."

The push for SCNT will be strong in the coming years. Because the most vocal critics of this research are from the anti-abortion community, many pro-choice advocates are reluctant to get involved with this debate for fear of lending support to the wide anti-choice agenda. Although there are those who have deliberately confused this issue, whatever the practical purpose of egg collection may be, it is important to insist that health concerns for women not take a back seat.

> "The best part is the response I get from couples who receive my eggs. They make me feel so special."

Egg Donation Brings Joy to Women

"Heidi" and "Tawni," interviewed by Nell Bernstein

In the following selection two ordinary women discuss their positive experiences with egg donation. First, a store manager, "Heidi," tells journalist Nell Bernstein about being an egg donor. The process is stressful, "Heidi" says, but she has never regretted it. Helping others to have children is deeply rewarding, she says, not so much for the money but for the gratitude of the parents she donates to. "Tawni," a thirty-three-year-old grocery clerk, had a different experience—she became a surrogate mother carrying donated eggs. Surrogacy is also a stressful process, "Tawni" says, but she has found it rewarding enough to undergo the procedure three times. Both women agree that the rewards of helping others to have children greatly outweigh the inconveniences. Nell Bernstein is a journalist who writes mostly about women's issues. She is also the author of All Alone in the World, *a book about children of incarcerated parents.*

Nell Bernstein, "The Incredible Choice I Made," *Marie Claire*, vol. 9, September 2002, pp. 170–175. Reproduced by permission.

As you read, consider the following questions:

1. What were the worst side effects of egg donation, according to "Heidi"?
2. How does "Heidi" feel about herself after donating eggs seven times?
3. What difficult choice did the parents of "Tawni"'s third surrogate pregnancy face?

[Heidi:] I first learned about egg donation [in 1998], when my sister was looking into becoming a surrogate. I thought it was such a neat idea. I have two little boys, ages 10 and 6, and they are the best things that ever happened to me. I thought giving a child to a couple in need would be a very rewarding experience.

I've donated eggs seven times now. I have to go through days of fertility shots, which my husband gives me, and then have my eggs retrieved under general anesthesia. After that, the eggs are fertilized in a lab, and the resulting embryos are implanted in the mom-to-be. The fifth time was the worst. I created 48 eggs in one cycle, and my body went through something like a mini menopause. It was terrible. I got hot flashes and gained 20 pounds. I looked like I was five-months pregnant. There are also a few medicines that really burn, but I have never said to myself, Why am I doing this? I know why I'm doing it: I love to help people.

There are four children out there right now who were born of my eggs. I've met some of their parents, but I have mixed feelings about meeting the kids. I think it would be kind of scary. What would the child think? And how would my own kids feel?

Donor but Not Mother

One couple sent me pictures, and their baby looks just like me. That's a strange feeling, but I didn't carry the baby, I didn't raise it—I'm not the mom. I have my two little guys, so I know what being a mom really is.

Safeguards at Every Step

"The egg donation process at certified centers takes various steps. The potential recipient and the sperm of the would-be father are tested to make sure a pregnancy is viable. Donors are screened psychologically and for infectious diseases and take hormones to induce the production of several eggs, while the recipient takes hormones to get her menstrual cycle in sync with the donor's. The recipient undergoes anesthesia when eggs are retrieved. The eggs are then prepared for fertilization in a lab. Two to three days after they are fertilized, the embryos are ready to be transferred to the recipient's uterus."

Sue Zeidler, Washington Post, *November 25, 2006.*

When I did my first cycle . . . , I got paid $2500. The fee has gone up over the years. I just got chosen by a new couple, and this time, I'll be paid $8000. I'm not doing it for the money, but it has helped a lot. I've made about $30,000 in all—enough to start saving to buy a house.

The best part is the response I get from couples who receive my eggs. They make me feel so special. One couple had a nursery all ready for years. They'd been through one egg donor, a surrogate, and another egg donor, and finally succeeded with me. That was the greatest.

Is it worth it? Of course. Children are the best thing in the whole world, and helping other people have children is a great gift. I'm an angel—that's how I feel inside. . . .

["Tawni":] When I was 18, a doctor told me an infection had affected my fallopian tubes, and I wouldn't be able to have kids. That broke my heart, because I loved children and really wanted to be a mom someday.

But when I met my husband, I miraculously got pregnant with my daughter. And 10 months after she was born, I got pregnant with my second. So, when I heard about surrogacy on the news, I just felt compelled to do it—I knew it was the right thing. My family was naturally concerned for my health, but in the end, they were all supportive.

I contacted Egg Donation, Inc., and the Center for Surrogate Parenting, both in Encino, CA, and things just snowballed from there. The center sends out profiles of people looking for a surrogate. I picked a couple; the woman was not able to carry a child because she'd had radiation treatments for cancer. But, importantly, she was still able to produce her own eggs. I would not want to use my own; that would be too close for me. And I guess it was meant to be—we got pregnant on the very first try.

Painful Procedures

You have to get a lot of shots when you're trying to get pregnant as a surrogate. One is to suppress your own eggs, and then, close to the time of the embryo transfer, big needles that hurt are used to inject progesterone, which helps build up the lining of your uterus so the embryos will implant. It's very difficult physically—and mentally. You have to go into surrogacy with no doubt in your mind that it's that couple's baby—otherwise, it's too hard.

As the months progress, I keep the mother apprised of her baby's progress. For example, if the baby kicks a lot, I'll call the mom and say, "Tell your daughter to be nice to me!" I always call after every doctor appointment, and the parents can call my doctor and ask any questions.

Right after that first baby was born, my doctor wanted to hand her to me. I said, "No, give her to the mom." I know the importance of holding your baby those first few critical minutes.

Later, when I was pregnant with my own third child, the same couple called me again and asked if I would carry another for them. I said, "Sorry, the womb is occupied. As soon as it's free, I'll let you know!"

I've been a surrogate three times so far. Of course, I don't do it just for the money, but I was paid $10,000 for my first surrogacy, $14,000 for the second, and $26,000 for the third—which was triplets! I wasn't too shocked, because that's a common risk when you use fertility drugs. Not only was I thrilled for the couple, but my husband and I were able to pay off our own debt and put money into savings.

My son was 11 months old when I got pregnant with my second surrogate baby. After that, I waited a while, but I felt so compelled to do it again. I never wanted another woman to feel the hopelessness I'd felt when I thought I couldn't conceive. I met a new couple who had been trying for years, and I got pregnant on the third try.

Happy to Help

At six weeks, the doctors told me it was twins. The next week, I went for another ultrasound—and that's when I learned it was actually triplets. I knew it could be risky, but my only real fear was that the couple would choose to "reduce" the pregnancy, which basically means removing an embryo to give the others a better chance of survival. Ultimately, I'd have had to abide by their decision, but it would have been so difficult.

The mom was more shocked than I was that she now had three babies, not two. But, thankfully, she never considered reduction. At the end of the pregnancy, I had to spend six weeks in the hospital on total bed rest. It was hard being away from my family, but I knew that what I was doing was very important.

The triplets were born at 31 weeks, about a month premature. They spent six weeks in the hospital. I pumped a liter of breast milk every day to help their growth.

The first time the parents saw the babies, it was awesome. I was sad to let them go, but it's great to be able to help others.

Everyone thinks I'm crazy. But when you find something you can do that makes so many people happy, you want to do it again and again.

> *"Rather than let [reproductive] technologies . . . violate women's bodies, dignity and integrity, let us work . . . towards ensuring the future of human rights and human equality."*

Future Harms of Reproductive Technologies Are Worth Opposing Now

Sujatha Jesudason

In the following viewpoint, Sujatha Jesudason recounts the violence and repression inflicted on women in her native India, ranging from infanticide to spousal abuse. That traditional violence may find new expression in reproductive technologies, she warns. Emerging genetic technologies, such as preimplantation embryonic screening tests, have the potential to harm women's health, Jesudason claims. One of her concerns is that as technology permits an increasing range of parental choices, women's eggs and other body parts may increasingly be demanded to provide material for genetic enhancements of offspring. She also fears that children and their mothers will be valued by new, ar-

Sujatha Jesudason, "The Future of Violence Against Women: Human Rights & the New Genetics," Center for Genetics and Society, February 21, 2006. www.genetics-and-society.org. Reproduced with permission from the Women's Funding Network.

tificial standards of worth in keeping with available genetic enhancements. Sujatha Jesudason is program director for gender, justice, and human genetics at the Center for Genetics and Society in California.

As you read, consider the following questions:

1. What, according to Jesudason, are the raw materials of reproductive technologies?
2. Why does the author call reproductive technologies violence against women?
3. What interpretation of the final goal of reproductive technologies does Jesudason endorse?

I was born into a culture that embraces confusing messages about the worth and value of women. I grew up in an India where a woman such as Indira Gandhi could become a formidable leader, and yet female infants were routinely killed or starved because they were deemed less valuable than boys. This contradiction played out in my family where smart and competent women who made a difference in the world continued to live with men who abused them, or attempted suicide when their husbands left them. The female role models in my life oscillated between these radical extremes: powerful agents and valueless victims. For as much as I have resisted, this confusion has been a central struggle in my life; I have worked to believe that there is a place for me in this world, that I have a right to enjoyment and happiness, that I matter, and that I have the power to make a difference.

I began working to end violence against women nearly fifteen years ago when I realized that violence is one of the key tools of women's oppression. Not only does this violence literally beat us into submission but, like female infanticide, it inscribes messages of powerlessness, worthlessness and vulnerability onto our bodies, minds and spirits. For many women, this kind of physical and emotional vulnerability begins early and carries through into adulthood, when we struggle to understand how we matter, that we have bodily and emotional integrity, and that we deserve respect and have rights.

Biotech as Violence

As future science and biotechnology, in the form of stem cell research and reproductive genetic technologies, started insistently knocking at our public door, I started to think about the future forms of violence against women. Women's bodies and women's eggs are the raw materials of these new human biotechnologies—what forms of violence are they and will they perpetuate against women, and against future generations? While there have been many beneficial reproductive technological developments, we are also at a cross-roads where many of the technologies currently in use and under consideration—sex selection, pre-implantation genetic diagnosis, reproductive cloning and inheritable genetic modification—have the potential to endanger women's health and, moreover, threaten basic notions of human equality and human rights.

If we consider the different kinds of reproductive screening technologies promoted in the U. S. today, we can see the kind of troubling questions these technologies raise for women. Women's bodies are increasingly medicalized in these processes now, and women are under increasing pressures to produce particular kinds of children, whether they be of a particular sex or ability.

What's equally disquieting is that some of these practices are market-driven. Sex selection processes like MicroSort, a form of pre-conception sperm sorting, are being advertised as "family balancing" and "gender diversity" innocently asking, "Do you want to choose the gender of your next baby?" Technologies such as amniocentesis and pre-implantation genetic diagnosis have long been controversial among disability rights advocates, raising concerns about the normalization of selection processes and eugenic notions of desirable and undesirable traits. As these technologies develop, there are many who advocate that they be used not only for cures, but also for enhancement. They see no problem with women's eggs and genetic material being harvested and manipulated to modify future generations for specific eye color, faster-twitch muscles, increased intelligence, decreased need for sleep, narrower emotional capacity (to prevent depression), or any other futuristic notion of what a "better" human being should look like, act like or feel.

Questions of Worth

As the new reproductive and genetic technologies continue to develop, which messages will be programmed into women's minds, bodies and spirits as mothers? What about future generations of women in terms of their value, worth and power in the world? Will a woman's worth be determined by the "perfection" of the children she bears? Will a baby's value be determined by the amount of money a parent can spend to "buy" the screening processes and genetic modifications? Will a girl's worth be measured by how well she fits the gendered stereotypes in her parents' mind when they selected for her using MicroSort? What will be the value and worth of "designed" children, and of children whose parents could not afford to pre-select the traits of their children?

As somebody who has worked for many years in domestic violence prevention, particularly in the South Asian American community, I am careful about what I label as violence. With clear memories of broken and bloody bodies, I hesitate to call every violation of a woman's dignity and integrity a form of violence. And yet I watch as international scandals break out about the buying and selling of women's eggs for research with no discussion of women's health and safety concerns or the reduction of women's lives and bodies to their biological materials. We are looking at one of the new forms of violence against women.

Sexism Embedded in Technology

"Since new reproductive technologies harm women both individually and collectively, feminists would deny that reproductive assistance should be considered a moral right. Even if we extended the definition of moral rights to include the wants and desires of individuals, we would have to assume that every woman ultimately desires to have a child of her own. This assumption is a reiteration of the sexist view that a woman's duty is child-birth and child-rearing."

Lisa Di Valentino,
Women's Issues and Social Empowerment, *1998.*
www.geocities.com/divalentino/rights.html.

It is in the violence against women movement that we have developed our most organized and consistent voice in our struggle for women's respect, dignity and power in the world. We have named the violence and work to stop it. And this is the movement [that] continues to most clearly advocate and organize for women's bodily integrity and human rights, and that believes in the power, worth and well-being of women and girls.

Market-Driven Eugenics

As I think about the perilous potentials of genetic and reproductive technologies, I am deeply concerned about what they may imply for future forms of violence against women in the genetic age. Eugenics has a long track record of targeting women; sterilization, incarceration, and rape are but a few of the ways we have been used as guinea pigs and selected out of existence. This new form of eugenics will also target women's bodies, integrity and fertility. In the past, eugenics movements—movements that have tried to "breed better human beings"—have been mostly state sponsored. While the eugenic practices of Nazi Germany most often come to mind, there were significant eugenic programs of sterilization, segregation and immigration restrictions in the early 1900s in the U.S. Now, however, we face the possibility of a market-based eugenics, where individuals in the marketplace could seek to either eliminate or promote particularly "desireable" or "undesireable" genetic characteristics through genetic screening, sex selection, gene therapies and genetic modification.

Do we have a language and a conceptual framework to articulate what these technologies will do to women's bodies, women's rights, and the value of women? We need to understand the kind of platforms of doubt and vulnerability this kind of normalization and selection will program into our culture and into our relationships with each other. And we need to start talking about the kind of violence and violation that will be done to women's bodies in the name of these technologies—the kind of eugenic violence and even genocide that might get practiced against particular groups of people, whether they be girl babies in India and China, Down's syndrome children in the U.S., or the "unperfect" children of the future. What will be our message to women and children if we start designing children? What kind of conditional love are we creating and what kind of inequality are we coding into our bodies and our selves?

Threat to Equality

Beyond the violations of human rights perpetuated by these technologies, these market-driven eugenics have the potential to end the human community as we know it. Some biotech advocates envision a world of "genetic castes" with the "Gen-Rich" and "Naturals", where people who are wealthy enough to afford genetic modifications will rule over those who are not modified. These technologies hold the potential to encode existing social inequalities into genetic make-up. Race and racism will no longer be merely social problems, but will be genetically engraved into our bodies. Will it be possible to ensure human equality, democracy and human rights for genetically and biologically different human beings?

So, what can we do about this? In addition to policies that ban reproductive cloning, inheritable genetic modification, and the marketing of selection procedures, we also need to start social and public discussions of the implications of these technologies. These decisions cannot be left up to scientists, biotechnology corporations and policy wonks; they need to be made by people and, in particular, women and the international community.

One route into these discussions is those old-fashioned consciousness-raising groups that characterized the beginning of the second wave of feminism. In such venues we need to talk about human rights and values in these intimate, personal decisions. Just like we did with domestic violence, sexual assault, and sexual harassment, our conversations with other women can turn private struggles into public and social problems. The new reproductive and genetic technologies raise all kinds of complicated and confusing questions—ethically, morally and socially. If we can share our doubts and confusions with each other, we can gain clarity about the broader social powers at play. We need to reflect more deeply on the values and worth we will encode in the bodies of women and in future generations.

A Need for Limits

How do we define what it means to be human in the genetic age? Who decides who is worthy of living? Who decides if we human beings need "enhancement" and at what price to women's bodies and lives? Without regulation or oversight, these technologies, will violate our fundamental human rights and the very foundation of human equality that makes possible the functioning of any democracy. We need to ensure that the rights of women, children and all humans are respected, protected and guaranteed.

In India the ethical and political understanding of these new human biotechnologies is much clearer. I could not say it any better than the Saheli Women's Resource Centre:

> The final goal of reproductive engineering appears to be the manufacture of a human being to suit exact specifications of physical attributes, class, caste, colour and sex. Who will decide these specifications? We have already seen how sex-determination has resulted in the elimination of female fetuses. The powerless in any society will get more disempowered with the growth of such reproductive technologies.

Over time, many women have been the target of eugenic practices—poor women, women of color, queer women, women with disabilities. The new reproductive and genetic technologies hold the potential for both great promise and great danger for women, our bodies and our communities. Rather than let these technologies slip down the slope of becoming the next tools of violence that violate women's bodies, dignity and integrity, let us work together in thoughtful and ethical ways towards ensuring the future of human rights and human equality.

Periodical Bibliography

The following articles have been selected to supplement the diverse views presented in this chapter.

Danville (KY) Advocate-Messenger
"Author, Husband Win Parental Rights to Baby," December 15, 2005. www.amnews.com/public_html/?module=displaystory&story_id=18236&format=html.

John Gillott
"IVF Babies: Life Chances," *Spiked Online*, June 24, 2003. www.spiked-online.com/Articles/00000006DE17.htm.

John Hanna
"Court to Consider Whether Sperm Donor Has Parental Rights," *Wichita (KS) Eagle*, November 27, 2006. www.kansas.com/mld/kansas/news/state/16110911.htm.

Jennifer J. Kurinczuk
"Safety Issues in Assisted Reproduction Technology," *Human Reproduction*, May 2003. http://humrep.oxfordjournals.org/cgi/content/full/18/5/925.

Beezy Marsh
"Fertility at Risk from IVF Drugs," *Telegraph* (London), December 4, 2006. www.smh.com.au/news/world/fertility-at-risk-from-ivf-drugs/2006/12/03/1165080815514.html.

Jan Nunn
"What I Feel About I.V.F.," Author'sDen.com, January 21, 2004. www.authorsden.com/visit/viewarticle.asp?AuthorID=17840.

Regnum News Agency
"Surrogate Mother Gave Birth to Triplets," December 14, 2005. www.regnum.ru/english/559843.html.

Sherman J. Silber
"Evaluation and Treatment of Male Infertility," *Clinical Obstetrics and Gynecology*, December 2000. www.clinicalobgyn.com.

Carly Zander
"Risk for Egg Donors Greatly Reduced Through Medical Protocol Developed by Las Vegas Infertility Specialist," *SIRM*, November 30, 2006. www.send2press.com/newswire/2006-11-1130-003.shtml

CHAPTER 2

What Ethical Issues Arise in Reproductive Technologies?

Chapter Preface

The ethical dilemmas presented by reproductive technologies are manifold. Some ethicists condemn the practice of paying for donated eggs, for example. They argue that only women in dire circumstances are likely to respond to such incentives and that therefore the practice amounts to exploitation of the poor. Others focus on the consent of the child, which obviously cannot be obtained for a procedure that results in the child's birth. Still others accuse fertility clinics of unfairly exploiting the hopes of couples with little chance of conceiving, who end up bearing only monumental bills to pay for the attempt.

One ethical question towers over all the others, however: what special consideration, if any, should be given to embryos? The deliberate creation of embryos through artificial intervention is the hallmark of reproductive technologies. The most prevalent form of fertility treatment—in vitro fertilization, or IVF—results not only in the hoped-for baby (when successful) but also in the creation of numerous extra embryos that are typically put into long-term storage, then destroyed if not used. This horrifies people who regard embryos as human beings. They regard any procedure that involves the deliberate destruction of embryos as being tantamount to murder.

On the other hand, for those who look on embryos as no more than a clump of cells with the mere potential to become a human baby, there is a very different kind of moral issue at stake. For the latter, the issue is not whether the creation of spare embryos is somehow wrong, but rather the impediment to using those embryos to further medical research that might cure a range of diseases and ailments. Embryos, proponents claim, are an indispensable source of stem cells for this type of research.

The dividing line on the question of embryos tends to coincide with religious views. As the Pew Research Center observes, "Religious commitment is the most important factor influencing attitudes of opponents of stem cell research." For those whose faith dictates the view that a new human person is created at conception, embryos are morally indistinguishable from babies. For those whose religions take a different view of "ensoulment," "quickening," or, in everyday terms, the beginning of human personhood, opinions on the moral status of embryos vary. Many mainstream Protestant and Jewish authorities differ with Catholicism on the latter's position that embryos are equivalent to persons. On the other hand, Evangelical Protestants by and large favor the use of in vitro fertilization but oppose the use of leftover embryos for research. Islamic clerics are divided on the question with some strongly in favor and some adamantly opposed.

Secular ethicists have their own divisions, of course, but the majority appear to favor treating embryos as something more than mere tissue but less than persons. This moral bracketing opens the door to IVF and to stem cell research, but within limits that in some way or other demonstrate respect for the embryo. As yet there appears to be no societal consensus on how this could best be achieved. The authors in the following chapter offer opinions on these issues.

*"The use of spare embryos [for research]
will lead to a more general and societal
decrease of respect for embryos."*

Embryos Deserve the Moral Status of Persons

Rogeer Hoedemaekers

*In the following selection, ethicist Rogeer Hoedemaekers rebuts a
wide variety of arguments in favor of using embryos for research.
Rejecting what he terms "moral ingenuity," he favors settling any
uncertainties in favor of granting full moral status to human
embryos at any stage. Hoedemaekers claims that nearly everyone
agrees that embryos should have at least some moral status.
Given that, he argues, attempts to justify destruction of embryos
for other purposes are misplaced. Rogeer Hoedemaekers is an
ethics researcher in the School of Medical Sciences of Radboud
University Nijmegen in the Netherlands. He holds a doctorate in
bioethics, with a specialization in issues surrounding genetic
screening.*

As you read, consider the following questions:

1. What conclusion does the author draw from scientific
   uncertainty about when embryonic cells are no longer
   totipotent?

Rogeer Hoedemaekers, "Human Embryos, Human Ingenuity, and Government Policy,"
Ethics and Medicine: An International Journal of Bioethics, summer 2003. Reproduced
by permission.

2. How does Hoedemaekers view the intention of an embryo's creators?

3. What obstacle stands in the way of justifying use of embryos to cure disease, in the author's opinion?

On the basis of what is now scientifically known about the beginning of human life it is justified to mark the process of fertilization as the beginning of new human life—a process which takes about 24 hours and begins with the penetration of the ovum by the sperm and ends with the creation of a new genome. Crucial in this process is the moment of recombination (fusion) of the genetic material of both gametes into a new and unique genome which starts a programmed gradual development towards the completion of becoming a new human individual.

An embryo can therefore be defined as a cell or group of cells which is totipotent [a cell with the capacity to form an entire organism] and which—in its natural environment—has the potential to develop into a human individual. At present a new genome cannot only be created in the womb, but also in petri [dishes] through various techniques. Creation of new human life through [somatic] cell nuclear transfer is the most recent technique, where the genetic material in a cell nucleus is transferred to an egg from which the original nucleus has been removed. Through electrofusion a new cell is created which is totipotent and which, in an appropriate environment, has the potential to develop into a human individual. Such a cell falls within the definition given above and deserves the same protection as other embryos.

An important question for human embryonic stem cell research is at what stage of development the growing cluster of cells is not totipotent anymore. A totipotent cell can, in principle, be separated from this cluster and develop into any of the many different types of body cells. Also, when it is brought into the appropriate environment (uterus), it can develop into a new human individual. Totipotent cells can therefore also be regarded as embryos. They must be distinguished from pluripotent cells, however. These cells can still differentiate into many, but not all, types of body cells or tissue, and more importantly, they do not have the potential anymore to develop into a new human being. . . .

Too Much Uncertainty

When a cell is isolated from the developing embryo which is not totipotent anymore, it cannot be regarded as an embryo and can therefore be used for research purposes—if the separation does not lead to the destruction of the source. The present state of the art does not justify a definitive conclusion with regard to the moment the embryonic cells are not totipotent anymore. It is unknown whether an isolated cell from a human embryo at the eight-cell stage will develop into a new human being. It is assumed that in the eight-cell stage five cells are involved in the development of the trophoblast (the layer of cells in the embryo which will establish relation with the uterus) and three cells which will eventually develop into the embryo proper. This would imply that cells at the eight-cell stage are already differentiating and cannot be termed totipotent anymore, but until now there is no certainty about this. This uncertainty should therefore lead to great restraint in using these cells.

False Distinctions

Moral ingenuity has assigned to some types of embryos a greater moral status (therefore deserving of more protection) than others. For example, a distinction has been made between 'spare' embryos, which remain 'unused' after fertility treatment, and embryos especially created for research purposes. Proponents of embryonic research point to the many embryos left over from an IVF [in vitro fertilization] procedure. They argue that from a moral point of view it is better

Doomed Embryos Deserve Dignity, Too

"They are destined to die by our will and choice. What follows? Not that we should feel free to use them, but rather that, having condemned them to their fate, we should refrain from the added indignity of regarding them as handy research material. We cannot pretend that they simply are dying—as if that were a natural fact independent of our will and choice. First we decide that they must die. Then we say that, since they're destined to die anyway, we might as well gain some good from that tragedy. Looked at in this light, the argument seems inherently corrupting."

Gilbert Meilaender, Weekly Standard, *August 26, 2002.*

to use these supernumerary embryos than to create embryos especially for research. At first sight this seems a reasonable approach, but this position can be rejected for a number of reasons.

Improvements in fertility treatments will reduce the number of spare embryos and the number of embryos potentially 'available' for research will therefore become smaller. It is therefore reasonable to assume that use of spare embryos is only the first step, leading inevitably to the creation of embryos for research when the number of spare embryos is insufficient.

It could be tempting to create a few extra embryos in an IVF procedure, which could then be used for research after the procedure is completed.

If the creation of a new genome is taken as the starting point of a programmed development of an embryo into a human being (see above), a distinction in moral status between spare embryos and embryos created for research purposes cannot be defended. From this it follows that, once the use of spare embryos is accepted, it will be difficult to stop the creation of new embryos for research, precisely because there is no difference in moral status between spare embryos and embryos created for research.

More importantly, the expectation is that the use of spare embryos will lead to a more general and societal decrease of respect for embryos. This expectation is felt to be real. In the past, acceptance of more inefficient IVF procedures implied permission to create a greater number of embryos than truly necessary. This led to a request to use the extra embryos for research purposes. Permission would imply further instrumental use of embryos. The next step now is to create embryos especially for research purposes. . . .

The Genome Is What Counts

Another distinction in moral status is made between human embryos used for reproduction and embryos used for therapeutic reasons. The argument is that—when used for research purposes—these embryos do not have the potential to become human beings because they are not transferred to the uterus. This distinction in moral status can also be rejected. The crucial point is that the moral status of the embryo cannot depend on the intentions of the creators. An embryo created in the dish possesses a new genome and has the potential to become a new human being. It is an act of the human will that it is not placed into the appropriate environment (the uterus) and that this potential will not be fulfilled. Accepting a different moral status for research embryos would imply that the moral status of the embryo is dependent on the arbitrary intentions of the scientist. The implication of this position for spare embryos is that at the very moment an embryo is not selected for implantation its moral status changes. By analogy, can parents who are expecting a baby change the moral status of a developing embryo or fetus simply by wishing for or having an abortion? This position denies the intrinsic worth of all developing forms of human life. In a similar form of reasoning a difference in moral status is grounded on the probability that an embryo will develop into a new human being. This probability is greater if it is implanted in the uterus, and this embryo has therefore a higher moral status than an embryo which is not transferred. Obviously, here, too, the moral status is dependent on the intentions of the 'creator' to transfer the embryo to its natural environment or not.

A distinction in moral status has also been based on different processes of creation. Embryos can be created by traditional fertilization techniques or by cell nuclear transfer. It is argued that embryos created by cell nuclear transfer are not intended to develop into a new human individual. This argument not only disregards the various attempts to clone human beings, but is also based on the assumption that the intentions of the 'creator' are decisive for the moral status of the human embryo. The crucial moral moment is, however, the creation of a new embryo, which in principle can become a new individual. It is man who decides what happens and in which kind of environment an embryo is placed. These arbitrary decisions cannot determine the moral status of the embryo.

The 'appeal to nature' argument, put forth in support of the Embryo Protection Act, can also be rejected. The argument is that many embryos are lost in the uterus also. This apparently also justifies the destruction of embryos for research purposes. This argument is rejected because the oversight is that man is not morally responsible for natural processes in the womb. He is responsible, however, for the creation of embryos in the dish and their subsequent development as well as for their intentional destruction.

For our purposes it is noteworthy that both proponents and opponents do assign moral status to the embryo. [Bioethicist Gilbert Meilaender states,] 'Many parties to the debate, at least, do agree that the embryo should be treated with respect'. So the difference is not between embryos with no moral status at all and full moral status, but between embryos with full moral status and embryos with a somewhat lesser status—a difference of degree. The implicit assumption underlying the attempts to create differences in moral status is that it is easier to weigh the moral value of embryos against the interests of future patients. But this is an approach which presents considerable difficulties. . . .

No Justifiable Destruction

Research with human embryonic stem cells is undertaken because of their (assumed) 'potential for significant advances in tissue transplantation, pharmaceutical testing and embryology' [according to the Geron Ethics Advisory Board]. Destruction of a human embryo is not justifiable for those who seek full protection for the embryo. But those who accept a lesser moral status face a difficult question: which (therapeutic) interests have more weight than the protection of early forms of human life? Such a weighing of interests is complex.

In much of the present moral debate it is assumed that the interests of (future) patients with degenerative and debilitating diseases outweigh a lesser moral status of embryos. Embryos can therefore be justified for use in medical research or for new therapies. It proves very difficult, however, to determine precisely which therapeutic aims are weighty enough to morally justify instrumental use of embryos for research. Precise and concrete criteria to determine this have not yet been offered and until now the balancing of interests tends to be intuitive, precisely because the specific moral status of embryos has not been defined yet, and, consequently, the degree of moral respect they deserve. It is not clear in advance which forms of research are important enough. Therefore there is a real possibility that, because of lack of criteria, there is a more or less ad hoc solution, subject to scientific, financial, or patient pressure.

"The fact that every person began life as an embryo does not prove that embryos are persons."

Embryos Do Not Deserve the Moral Status of Persons

Michael J. Sandel

The use of embryos in stem cell research raises fears of a wider use in reproductive technologies, says Michael J. Sandel in the following selection. Human embryos do deserve a certain level of respect, he admits. All the same, Sandel argues, those who would equate embryos with human persons are mistaken. Embryos are as different from people as acorns are from oak trees, he says. Sandel points out that few people treat the claim that embryos are people seriously. There are no funerals for the many embryos that naturally fail to develop. Michael J. Sandel is the Anne T. and Robert M. Bass professor of government at Harvard University. He is a former member of the President's Council on Bioethics.

As you read, consider the following questions:

1. How does Sandel compare an old-growth forest with an embryo?

2. What would the implication for infertility treatments be if embryos were treated as persons, according to the author?

3. How can Congress, according to Sandel, head off the fears of a slippery slope to exploitation of embryos?

At first glance, the case for federal funding of embryonic stem-cell research seems too obvious to need defending. Why should the government refuse to support research that holds promise for the treatment and cure of devastating conditions such as Parkinson's disease, Alzheimer's disease, diabetes, and spinal cord injury? Critics of stem-cell research offer two main objections: some hold that despite its worthy ends, stem-cell research is wrong because it involves the destruction of human embryos; others worry that even if research on embryos is not wrong in itself, it will open the way to a slippery slope of dehumanizing practices, such as embryo farms, cloned babies, the use of fetuses for spare parts, and the commodification of human life.

Acorns and Oaks Differ

Neither objection is ultimately persuasive, though each raises questions that proponents of stem-cell research should take seriously. Consider the first objection. Those who make it begin by arguing, rightly, that biomedical ethics is not only about ends but also about means; even research that achieves great good is unjustified if it comes at the price of violating fundamental human rights. For example, the ghoulish experiments of Nazi doctors would not be morally justified even if they resulted in discoveries that alleviated human suffering.

Few would dispute the idea that respect for human dignity imposes certain moral constraints on medical research. The question is whether the destruction of human embryos in stem-cell research amounts to the killing of human beings. The "embryo objection" insists that it does. For those who adhere to this view, extracting stem cells from a blastocyst is morally equivalent to yanking organs from a baby to save other people's lives.

Some base this conclusion on the religious belief that ensoulment occurs at conception. Others try to defend it without recourse to religion, by the following line of reasoning: Each of us began life as an embryo. If our lives are worthy of respect, and hence inviolable, simply by virtue of our humanity, one would be mistaken to think that at some younger age or earlier stage of development we were not worthy of respect. Unless we can point to a definitive moment in the passage from conception to birth that marks the emergence of the human person, this argument claims, we must regard embryos as possessing the same inviolability as fully developed human beings.

But this argument is flawed. The fact that every person began life as an embryo does not prove that embryos are persons. Consider an analogy: although every oak tree was once an acorn, it does not follow that acorns are oak trees, or that I should treat the loss of an acorn eaten by a squirrel in my front yard as the same kind of loss as the death of an oak tree felled by a storm. Despite their developmental continuity, acorns and oak trees are different kinds of things. So are human embryos and human beings. Sentient creatures make claims on us that nonsentient ones do not; beings capable of experience and consciousness make higher claims still. Human life develops by degrees.

Those who view embryos as persons often assume that the only alternative is to treat them with moral indifference. But one need not regard the embryo as a full human being in order to accord it a certain respect. To regard an embryo as a mere thing, open to any use we desire or devise, does, it seems to me, miss its significance as potential human life. Few would favor the wanton destruction of embryos or the use of embryos for the purpose of developing a new line of cosmetics.

Personhood is not the only warrant for respect. For example, we consider it an act of disrespect when a hiker carves his initials in an ancient sequoia—not because we regard the sequoia as a person, but because we regard it as a natural wonder worthy of appreciation and awe. To respect the old-growth forest does not mean that no tree may ever be felled or harvested for human purposes. Respecting the forest may be consistent with using it. But the purposes should be weighty and appropriate to the wondrous nature of the thing.

Embryos Lack Full Standing

The notion that an embryo in a petri dish has the same moral status as a person can be challenged on further grounds. Perhaps the best way to see its implausibility is to play out its full implications. First, if harvesting stem cells from a blastocyst were truly on a par with harvesting organs from a baby, then the morally responsible policy would be to ban it, not merely deny it federal funding. If some doctors made a practice of killing children to get organs for transplantation, no one would take the position that the infanticide should be ineligible for federal funding but allowed to continue in the private sector. If we were persuaded that embryonic stem-cell research were tantamount to infanticide, we would not only ban it but treat it as a grisly form of murder and subject scientists who performed it to criminal punishment.

Second, viewing the embryo as a person rules out not only stem-cell research, but all fertility treatments that involve the creation and discarding of excess embryos. In order to increase pregnancy rates and spare women the ordeal of repeated attempts, most in-vitro fertilization clinics create more fertilized eggs than are ultimately implanted. Excess embryos are typically frozen indefinitely or discarded. (A small number are donated for stem-cell research.) But if it is immoral to

"Well, it certainly looks like your DNA. How many times have I told you to wear gloves before touching anything?"

© CartoonStock.com

sacrifice embryos for the sake of curing or treating devastating diseases, it is also immoral to sacrifice them for the sake of treating infertility.

Third, defenders of in-vitro fertilization point out that embryo loss in assisted reproduction is less frequent than in natural pregnancy, in which more than half of all fertilized eggs either fail to implant or are otherwise lost. This fact highlights a further difficulty with the view that equates embryos and persons. If natural procreation entails the loss of some embryos for every successful birth, perhaps we should worry less about the loss of embryos that occurs in in-vitro fertilization and stem-cell research. Those who view embryos as persons might reply that high infant mortality would not justify infanticide. But the way we respond to the natural loss of embryos suggests that we do not regard this event as the moral or religious equivalent of the death of infants. Even those religious traditions that are the most solicitous of nascent human life do not mandate the same burial rituals and mourning rites for the loss of an embryo as for the death of a child. Moreover, if the embryo loss that accompanies natural procreation were the moral equivalent of infant death, then pregnancy would have to be regarded as a public health crisis of epidemic proportions; alleviating natural embryo loss would be a more urgent moral cause than abortion, in-vitro fertilization, and stem-cell research combined.

Research and Restrictions Possible

Even critics of stem-cell research hesitate to embrace the full implications of the embryo objection. President George W. Bush has prohibited federal funding for research on embryonic stem-cell lines derived after August 9, 2001, but has not sought to ban such research, nor has he called on scientists to desist from it. And as the stem-cell debate heats up in Congress, even outspoken opponents of embryo research have not mounted a national campaign to ban in-vitro fertilization or to prohibit fertility clinics from creating and discarding excess embryos. This does not mean that their positions are unprincipled—only that their positions cannot rest on the principle that embryos are inviolable.

What else could justify restricting federal funding for stem-cell research? It might be the worry, mentioned above, that embryo research will lead down a slippery slope of exploitation and abuse. This objection raises legitimate concerns, but curtailing stem-cell research is the wrong way to address them. Congress can stave off the slippery slope by enacting sensible regulations, beginning with a simple ban on human reproductive cloning. Following the approach adopted by the United

Kingdom, Congress might also require that research embryos not be allowed to develop beyond 14 days, restrict the commodification of embryos and gametes, and establish a stem-cell bank to prevent proprietary interests from monopolizing access to stem-cell lines. Regulations such as these could save us from slouching toward a brave new world as we seek to redeem the great biomedical promise of our time.

> "*I do not think that we need to sacralize gametes and embryos in order to make them 'untouchable' for research and commodification. Instead we should think about secular ways of protecting women (as well as men) from being objectified.*"

A Secular Regard for the Human Body Means Restricting Reproductive Technologies

Ingrid Schneider

In the following selection Ingrid Schneider argues from a feminist perspective that the sale or donation of human gametes is unethical. She says that secular ethics are enough to show that it is wrong to commodify eggs or sperm. Even donations are unacceptable, in Schneider's view, because there is great pressure on women to give. Schneider calls for a new ethic of inalienability of the body, which would effectively limit reproductive technology to helping couples use their own gametes to reproduce. Ingrid

Ingrid Schneider, "'Pro-Life' and 'Pro-Choice': Overcoming the Misleading Controversy," Gender and Justice in the Gene Age, October 10, 2003. www.gjga.org. Reproduced by permission of the author.

Schneider is a political scientist, at the Research Center on Biotechnology, Society, and the Environment (BIOGUM) at the University of Hamburg in Germany.

As you read, consider the following questions:

1. Why does Schneider believe there is no such thing as a woman's right to have a child?

2. Why do gametes deserve special status, in the author's view?

3. What is the key difference between male and female gametes, according to Schneider?

The challenges and conflicts raised by new genetic and reproductive technologies have often been overshadowed by old cleavages about abortion and women's right to choose. But framing the issues raised by the new technologies in either embryo-centric and "pro-life" terms or in terms of liberal self-determination does not do justice to women's needs nor to the political strategies feminists have opted for. Such a framing, moreover, is an impediment to building broader alliances.

I think it is necessary to emphasize differences that are of normative significance. Therefore it is important to distinguish between what needs to be kept apart—and to think together about what is inherently connected. . . .

The Child's Interest

Contraception and abortion are different than reproduction, because in reproduction a third party—a child—is (hoped to be) brought into existence.

As British biomedical philosopher Onora O'Neill has stated, while in the cases of contraception and abortion

> the aim of the woman or couple involved is not to reproduce: there is no need to consider the right, welfare or fu-

ture of any child, since no child will exist. But where the aim is to reproduce, appeals to individual or personal autonomy are much less convincing. Reproduction aims to create a dependent being, and reproductive decisions [must have as a primary goal to] offer adequate and lasting care and support to the hoped-for child.

Thus in matters of reproduction the best interests of a child and the relationship with the parents-to-be have to be taken into account, which limits an individual's autonomy in the traditional sense. . . .

Feminists have always emphasized the low baby take-home rates (around 15%) of IVF [in vitro fertilization] and the health risks for both women and children associated with the technologies.

But in many cases it seems that procreation nowadays is being framed in terms of a positive right, an entitlement. I think, however, that there *cannot* be an entitlement or *"right" to "have a child"*—who would be the legitimate addressee or focus of such a demand? Neither the state nor an individual man could be obliged to provide sperm to a woman to fulfill her wish for a child. An entitlement to have a child would go beyond that which can rightly be demanded and guaranteed. And even less can there be an *entitlement to a healthy child*. Individuals might claim a right not to be polluted or subjected to radiation in order to have a healthy child, thus to be protected from environmental harm. And a doctor is of course obliged to do his work *lege artis* [according to accepted medical rules]. However, the negative selection of a fetus according to norms of health certainly exceeds the medical mandate. . . .

Selective Abortion

There is a difference between the right not to carry an unwanted pregnancy to term (or, in other words, to decide whether or not to have a child) and the decision to abort because certain traits of the fetus have been discovered (or, bluntly speaking, because the "quality" is not sufficient).

Women's Bodies Exposed to Unknown Risks

"The long-term risks of fertility drugs are unknown. A few studies suggest that fertility drugs might increase a woman's risk for developing ovarian cancer later in life. Others do not show this link. At this time, no one knows for sure. . . . There are no firm rules about how many times a woman can donate her eggs, but there are several reasons why a program may limit repeat donations. For one thing, there are still unanswered questions about the possible long-term impact on a woman's health and fertility."

New York State Department of Health, "Becoming an Egg Donor,"
October 2002.

As feminists have learnt from discussions with people from the disability movements, there is a significant difference between the two. Selective abortion implies the affirmation of derogatory and negative cultural value judgments and norms. On the practical level, of course, this does not translate into an obligation to carry a pregnancy to term, but does mean that the widespread supply of prenatal diagnosis or testing as a screening method must be questioned. . . .

All these conflicts are exacerbated by the technique of Preimplantation Genetic Diagnosis (PGD). When this technique is employed, there is no longer an intimate, corporeal connection and bonding between the woman and an embryo (or fetus) as in pregnancy. Instead, there is a separation of the woman and the embryo, which has a (social and institutional) existence in the petri dish, in vitro. . . .

Embryonic stem cell research and human cloning require an enormous supply of oocytes [egg cells] and embryos, thus degrading women into "producers of raw material" for third parties. This scientifically created "need" calls for measures to meet the demand, either for financial or for emotional reasons. Both the commodification of egg and embryo donation, as well as the so-called "altruistic" donation, is—in my opinion—detrimental to the practical and strategic needs of women. . . .

False Gifts

One dichotomy is that between girl and commodity or—in the terms used to describe circulation—between the rules of gift exchange, which creates a never-ending chain of social relationships, bonds, obligations and reciprocity on the one hand and the rules of commodity exchange which is governed by contract and market competition on the other hand.

Often the connotations and conclusions drawn are that the gift is positive, a voluntary contribution, very much in line with Judaeo-Christian values of altruism, whereas the sale is negative and hence disapproved of.

I would like to argue, however, that it is not so easy to make the normative distinction between gift and sale—because *gifts* can imply very strong *obligations* in terms of gratitude, guilt and debt. These implications have led US sociologists Renee Fox and Judith Swazey to speak of "the tyranny of the gift". . . .

Moreover, as US feminist sociologist Janice Raymond has emphasized, the "gift" is often loaded with a strong gender bias, namely the cultural norm of the altruistic woman "who is infinitely giving and eternally accessible [which] derives from a social context in which women give and are given away, and from a moral tradition that celebrates women's duty to meet and satisfy the needs of others. . . . On a cultural level women are expected to donate themselves in the form of time, energy, and body"—and nowadays in the form of oocytes and embryos. . . .

Put Gametes Off-Limits

I would like to conclude by saying that what seems to be needed is a *new culture of inalienability* of the human body. Inalienability not only in terms of market-inalienability, but also in terms of absolute inalienability, in terms of non-procurement and non-circulation.

I do not think, that we need to *sacralize* gametes and embryos in order to make them "untouchable" for research and commodification. Instead we should think about *secular* ways of protecting women (as well as men) from being objectified and reified, and from subjecting themselves to instrumentalisation (or we might possibly go as far as to talk of alienation and expropriation of their reproductive potential).

In my opinion, gametes deserve a special status, because they are the material substrate of the human procreative potential—as such they represent fertility and potency. As a genealogical bridge between past and future, entailing relationships with our progenitors as well as with our present partners and with future generations, they are different from all other body substances. They not only carry half the chromosomal set, but they are also "half" insofar as they need a "counterpart" to become a child—and of course a woman willing to become pregnant and carry a pregnancy to term. . . .

Male/Female Differentiation

In my opinion, however, we should also focus on differences between male and female gametes, because gender in this aspect does make a difference: while sperm is more like a regenerative resource, which is relatively easy to provide, the extraction (or the "harvest," in the language of reproductive technology providers) of oocytes requires invasive, painful and risky medical procedures, involving hormonal stimulation and potential lesions during ova retrieval which can have negative effects on a woman's health. Therefore, it would be quite legitimate to have different attitudes and different legal regulations concerning sperm and oocyte donation. . . .

I think we must try and think about concepts and strategies to *set limits* to genetic and reproductive technologies without falling into the old traps set by conservative family ideologies, on the one hand, and by liberal technological optimism, scientism and uncritical allusions of control and progress, on the other. Our challenge is not to lapse into old separations but to commit ourselves to building new alliances.

*"Ultimately, decisions about how to use
or not use genomics in human reproduction will be determined ... by how
those uses fit into the fabric of rights
and interests of individual and social
choice and responsibility that particular societies recognize."*

A Secular Regard for Human Liberty Means Allowing Reproductive Technologies

John A. Robertson

*In the selection that follows, attorney John A. Robertson argues
for procreative liberty—that is, individual freedom to make
choices about reproduction, including use of reproductive technologies—under the banner of what he terms "modern traditionalism." This stance, Robertson explains, is modern in its acceptance of new technology but traditional in its regard for the
value of reproduction as a life goal of many people. Reproduction is so important to individuals that society should make a
strong presumption in its favor. Therefore, he concludes, reproductive technologies that help people to have healthy offspring*

John A. Robertson, "Procreative Liberty in the Era of Genomics," *American Journal of
Law & Medicine*, vol. 29, 2003, p. 439. © 2003 American Society of Law, Medicine &
Ethics. Reproduced by permission.

should be permitted. John A. Robertson holds the Vinson and El-
kins chair on the faculty of the University of Texas School of
Law. He has made a specialty of reproductive technology issues.

As you read, consider the following questions:

1. What does a biologic perspective show about human
   reproduction compared to that of other creatures, in
   Robertson's view?
2. According to the author, can an evolutionary perspective
   define the scope of reproductive liberty?
3. What, according to Robertson, would be grounds for
   limiting use of reproductive technologies?

Rather than adopt *strict traditionalism* that rejects almost
all selection technologies or *radical libertarianism* that rejects none, I adopt a *modern traditionalist* approach, which
looks closely at the reasons why choice about reproduction is
so important for individuals. The more closely an application
of genetic or reproductive technology serves the basic reproductive project of haploid gene transmission[1]—or its avoidance—and the rearing experiences that usually follow, the
more likely it is to fall within a coherent conception of procreative liberty deserving of special protection. At a certain
point, however, answers to questions about the scope or outer
limits of procreative liberty will depend upon socially consti-
tutive choices of whether reprogenetic procedures are viewed
as plausible ways to help individuals and couples transmit
genes to and rear a new generation.

The Importance of Reproduction

Why should procreative liberty have moral or legal right status? The answer might be so obvious that one wonders why
the question is even asked. But asking the question will help

1. *Haploid* refers to half the chromosomes found in an ordinary cell. In sexual reproduction each parent contributes a single set of chromosomes to the offspring, which
then carries a double set in all its cells, except the gametes it will use to reproduce.

us understand the interests and values that undergird the scope of procreative liberty and, by implication, help resolve conflicts that arise from its exercise. Quite simply, reproduction is an experience full of meaning and importance for the identity of an individual and her physical and social flourishing because it produces a new individual from her haploid chromosomes. If undesired, reproduction imposes great physical burdens on women, and social and psychological burdens on both men and women. If desired and frustrated, one loses the [as Shakespeare put it,] "defence 'gainst Time's scythe" that "increase" or replication of one's haploid genome provides, as well as the physical and social experiences of gestation, childrearing, and parenting of one's offspring. Those activities are highly valued because of their connection with reproduction and its role in human flourishing.

Good health in offspring is also greatly prized. Past cultures have sometimes exposed weaker or handicapped newborns to the elements, thus concentrating resources on those who are healthy. We serve some of the same interests by a strong commitment to the health of all children, such as elaborate neonatal intensive care units that go to great expense to save all newborns, and norms for treating all newborns no matter the cost or scope of their handicaps. Even though parental behavior, and social and legal norms are strongly committed to the well-being of children once they are born, parents strongly prefer having healthy offspring and may use mate or gamete selection, and screening of fetuses and embryos to serve that goal.

It is not surprising that an interlocking set of laws, norms, and practices exist that support reproduction. Deeply engrained social attitudes and practices celebrate the importance of family and children. Laws, ethical norms, and institutions protect and support human desires to have or avoid having offspring, and the rearing that follows. The deep psychological commitment one has to the well-being of one's offspring is

Eggs for Sale?

The United States is one of the many countries in which legislation and social norms proscribe the selling of body parts. It is also the capital of the genetic material market: No other nation trades in DNA so widely and freely. Hopeful mothers and cash-strapped college students have been trading cash for eggs for 20 years, calling the ova a "donation" and the money compensation for time and discomfort, thus avoiding the ban on sales.... Elsewhere, the laws reflect a surprising lack of consensus on the issue. In Germany, Denmark, and Italy, egg donation is completely illegal. In Israel, payment for eggs can cover only the direct expenses related to the procedure. In the U.K., eggs are classified as organs, and payment is banned.

Kerry Howley, Reason, *October 2006.*

reflected in the strong family and constitutional law protections for rearing rights and duties in biologic offspring, in special tort damages for loss of children and parents, in the law of rape, in the rise of an infertility industry, and in the wide acceptance of prenatal screening programs for the health of offspring. Many other social institutions and practices also support individual and social interests in producing healthy offspring who are fit to reproduce in turn. Strong protection of procreative liberty and family autonomy in rearing offspring is yet another way that social recognition of the importance of reproduction is shown.

Evolutionary Perspective

Although the importance of reproduction for individuals and society is intuitively accepted, the search for a deeper or more ultimate explanation of its importance might turn to evolutionary biology and psychology. A biologic perspective on human behavior suggests that reproductive success is as important an issue for humans as it is for other organisms. Whether gene, organism, group, or species is the unit of selection, natural selection selects those entities that are best suited to reproduce in the environments in which they exist. Although genes encoding sexuality and sexual attractiveness have not yet been identified, it is likely that many aspects of sexual reproduction reflect physical and perhaps even behavioral tendencies for reproductive success selected at earlier stages of human development.

Given the importance of culture and environment in shaping human behavior, one should be leery of attempting to explain all aspects of human reproductive decisions in evolutionary terms. Yet there are enough similarities between the reproductive challenges that humans and other organisms face to make further inquiry into the biologic basis of human reproduction worthwhile. Humans, like other sexually reproducing organisms, face specific challenges that differ for each sex. Typically, each sex faces the challenge of finding healthy members of the opposite sex with whom to mate and produce progeny. Because females typically have larger and fewer gametes that require internal fertilization, they use different strategies than males for identifying good mates and controlling their reproductive capacity. In either case, some selection of the gametes or reproductive partners may be necessary to maximize the chance of successful reproduction. Similarly, each sex must solve the problem of adequate nurture and protection of offspring, so that they may reproduce in turn.

The Desire for Healthy Offspring

As a result, it should be no surprise that many human reproductive choices and practices reflect efforts to have healthy offspring to carry genes into future generations. An evolutionary perspective on reproduction cannot itself define the limits or scope of procreative liberty. As the naturalistic fallacy teaches, no "ought" follows logically or inexorably from any "is" about the world. But a biologic perspective helps explain why reproductive urges are so powerful and widely respected, and why so many secondary norms, practices, and institutions have grown up around them.

Still, understanding how assisted reproductive and genetic technologies serve issues of reproductive fitness is relevant to the ethical, legal, and social debates that surround use of those techniques. The biological concept of reproductive fitness can help at an ultimate level explain what is intuitively felt and culturally protected, even though more proximate analyses are needed to resolve the ethical, legal, and social conflicts that use of reproductive technologies may pose. At the very least, an evolutionary perspective, if not directly supportive, makes comprehensible the *modern traditionalist* intuition that pro-creative liberty deserves respect because of the individual importance of having and rearing offspring in order to transmit genes to the next and later generations. . . .

Modern traditionalism strongly supports a liberty claim-right to use generic knowledge and techniques to have healthy offspring to nurture and rear. Genetic techniques that directly aim to serve those goals are usually ethically acceptable and should be legally available, for their use fits neatly into traditional understandings of why reproduction is valued. Access to them, however, could be limited if they imposed serious harms on the persons most directly affected by them. As genetic techniques grow in importance, providing access to persons without the means to obtain them will also be important.

Applying this perspective to four areas of current or future controversy, this article has shown that the most likely use of these techniques serve standard reproductive goals without causing undue harm to values of respect for prenatal life, the welfare of offspring, the status of women, or social equality.

"The [Catholic] Church teaches that IVF and human cloning are morally forbidden."

Intervention in God's Plan for Natural Reproduction Is Wrong

John B. Shea

In the selection that follows, John B. Shea explains and defends the Catholic Church's viewpoint on human reproductive issues. The Church, he says, takes an absolute stand against intervention in the natural reproductive process. In addition to forbidding contraceptive devices, he explains, the Church condemns in vitro fertilization (IVF) and human cloning. According to Shea, this is because IVF bypasses the act of conjugal union and violates the dignity of procreation. Additionally, he argues, a child born of such technology is deprived of a normal relationship with its natural parents. John B. Shea is a Toronto-based physician who writes extensively in defense of Catholic teachings on health issues.

John B. Shea, "What the Church Teaches about Human Reproduction," *Catholic Insight*, September 2006. © Copyright 2003-2006 by CatholicInsight.com. Reproduced by permission.

As you read, consider the following questions:

1. Why does the Catholic Church condemn 'the use of donated sperm or eggs in assisted reproduction, according to Shea?
2. Rather than being a product of technology, a child should be accepted as what, according to the author?
3. What happens to most children conceived by IVF, according to Shea?

The Catholic Church teaches that "the direct interruption of the generative process already begun, and, above all, directly willed and procured abortion, even if for therapeutic reasons, are absolutely excluded as licit means of regulating birth. Equally excluded . . . is direct sterilization, whether perpetual or temporary, whether of the man or the woman."

This teaching prohibits contraception by means of the condom; intrauterine device; vasectomy or tubal ligation; and chemical contraception by the use of oral contraceptives, morning after pills, or the administration of contraceptives by injection or in a skin patch. The reason for this prohibition is that contraception breaks the inseparable connection, willed by God and unable to be broken by man on his own initiative, between the unitive meaning and the procreative meaning of the conjugal act.

Contraception greatly dishonours marriage, the greatness of which is beautifully described by Dietrich von Hildebrand. "No natural human good has been exalted so high in the New Testament. No other good has been chosen to become one of the Seven Sacraments. No other has been endowed with the honor of participating in the establishment of the Kingdom of God. . . . The wonderful, divinely appointed relationship between the mysterious procreation of a new human being, and this most intimate communion of love . . . illuminates the grandeur and solemnity of this union. . . . Thus it is that in order to preserve the reverent attitude of the spouses toward the mystery of this union, this general connection between procreation and the communion of love must always be maintained."

Contraception Causes Promiscuity

History has clearly demonstrated how prescient Pope Paul VI [1897–1978, reigned 1963–1978] was, when he predicted that the practice of contraception would cause the man to lose respect for the woman, considering her a mere instrument of selfish enjoyment. The gigantic increase in the incidence of abortion and of sexually transmitted infections bears witness to the promiscuity that followed the legalization and wide availability of chemical contraceptives. The Pope also warned of the danger that public authorities, which take no heed of moral exigencies, would try to solve problems of the community by means illicit for married couples. Witness the worldwide promotion of contraception and abortion fostered by the United Nations today; and also, the mandatory one-child policy of the government of China.

Paul VI, in *Humanae vitae*, stated that "if, then, there are serious motives to space out births, which derive from the physical or psychological conditions of husband and wife, or from external conditions, the Church teaches that it is then licit to take into account the natural rhythms immanent in the generative functions, for the use of marriage in the infecund periods only, and in this way to regulate births without offending the moral principles which have been recalled earlier." Pius XII [pope from 1939 to 1958] taught that unless some serious circumstances arise, spouses are obliged to have children. However, he also teaches that it is moral for the spouses to limit their family size or even to refrain from having children altogether, if they have sufficiently serious reasons. He stated that "there are serious motives, such as those often mentioned in the so-called medical, eugenic, economic, and social 'indications,' that can except for a long time, perhaps even during the whole duration of the marriage, from the positive and obligatory carrying out of the act."

Gaudium et spes [a 1965 declaration promulgated by Paul VI] teaches that "among the married couples who thus fulfill their God-given mission, special mention should be made of those who after prudent reflection and common decisions, courageously undertake the proper upbringing of a large number of children." It also states that it is the duty of the parents, and of them alone, to decide on the number and spacing of children, and that they should take "into consideration their own good and the good of their children already born or yet to come, and ability to read the signs of the times and of their own situation, on the material and spiritual level, and finally, an estimation of the good of the family, of society, and of the Church." . . .

In Vitro Fertilization Condemned

A human being is normally brought into existence by the fertilization of an ovum by a sperm. This can be achieved by sexual intercourse, or in the laboratory by in vitro fertilization (IVF). Reproduction of a human being can also be achieved by cloning. There are many different methods of cloning that include nuclear transfer, embryo splitting, etc.

The Church teaches that IVF and human cloning are morally forbidden. Why? IVF between husband and wife is condemned because it is illicit in itself and in opposition to the dignity of procreation and the conjugal union. IVF in which the sperm or ovum of a third person is used, is also condemned, because, in addition, it violates the reciprocal commitment of spouses and shows a grave lack of regard for that essential property of marriage which is unity. It also deprives the child of her or his filial relationship with parental origins, can hinder the maturing of personal identity, can damage personal relationships within the family, and has repercussions on civil society.

IVF is neither in fact achieved nor positively willed as an expression and fruit of a specific act of conjugal union. The human embryo is treated as a product of technology and not as a gift of God. In its use and in the use of many other techniques of genetic engineering, a human person is objectively deprived of his or her proper perfection. Such fertilization establishes the domination of technology over the origin and destiny of the person. This domination is contrary to the dignity and equality that must be common to parents and children. Therefore, IVF and cloning are morally unacceptable.

Frequent Failures

Few of the children conceived by IVF are ever born. In each cycle, six to eight embryos are conceived. At most, two are implanted. The rest are either disposed of immediately, or are frozen and, eventually, most die. Only 25% of those conceived are implanted, and of them, only 20% are born. Therefore, only 5% of IVF embryos are born alive. The Australian bioethicist, Nicholas Tonti-Filippini, calculates that the chance of saving a given frozen human embryo by implantation is less than 2%.

Birth defects associated with ART [artifical reproductive technologies]: 4.9–7.2-fold increase in malignant tumour of the retina; 5% incidence of Beckwith-Wiedemann Syndrome (large tongue, predisposition to cancer); in Brazil, the incidence of cancer increased 117 times; cerebral palsy increased 1.4–1.7 times; 4-fold increase in developmental delay; premature birth increased 5.6 times; low birth rate increased 9.8 times and heart deformity increased 4 times.

To achieve IVF, a woman is given hormones to stimulate the development of many ova at the same time. This may cause Ovarian Hyper-stimulation Syndrome. Symptoms include nausea, vomiting, and breathing difficulty. In rare cases, blood clots, kidney or lung disease may occur and may be life threatening.

Dr. Thomas Hilgers' *FertilityCare System: Dr. Hilgers' Natural Procreative Technology* is a method of care that involves precise diagnosis of the hormonal causes of infertility, and its appropriate treatment. It is also morally acceptable as a way to help an infertile woman to conceive, and is two to three times more successful than IVF, at a fraction of the cost. One study on women who had previous failed IVF, showed a success rate of 36.2%. The Hilgers system has been shown to be up to 80% successful in helping women to have a successful pregnancy after they have suffered repeated miscarriages. It cuts the rate of premature birth in half, thus helping to reduce the incidence of brain damage.

"[The] blind acceptance of mixing ethics and medical science with religion is unacceptable, and it has got to stop."

Religion Should Not Interfere in Bioethics

George Dvorsky

In the following selection futurist George Dvorsky argues that religious interference in decisions about the ethics of reproductive technology is unwarranted and harmful. He argues that ethics have to evolve to keep up with scientific discoveries and technological possibilities. For example, brain death was not a concept available to people who lived in the era when the Bible was written, he notes. The moral absolutism of religious conservatives is particularly harmful, he claims, in an age when technology regularly prolongs and establishes life through artificial means. George Dvorsky is deputy editor of and a regular columnist for BetterHumans.com. He lives in Ontario, Canada.

As you read, consider the following questions:

1. What's wrong with the "wisdom of repugnance," in Dvorsky's view?

2. What, according to the author, is the source of moral absolutism?

3. How might giving full rights to embryos lead to every human cell having full rights?

It is now a criminal offense in Canada to engage in therapeutic cloning, to create an in vitro embryo for any purpose other than creating a human being (or for improving assisted human reproductive procedures), to maintain an embryo outside a woman's body for more than 14 days, to genetically manipulate embryos, to choose the gender of one's offspring, to sell human eggs and sperm and to engage in commercial surrogacy.

While I'm loath to admit it, and despite the merciful sanctioning of stem cell research (albeit under strict conditions), Canadian bioconservatives have clearly won a major battle here—and in this sense it's a *de facto* victory for religious interests. While not stated explicitly in the bill, it's quite obvious that C-6[1] upholds religious interpretations of personhood (namely the belief that life starts at conception) and theological injunctions against meddling in human biology and reproduction. . . .

This blind acceptance of mixing ethics and medical science with religion is unacceptable, and it has got to stop. For centuries, societies have known better than to let religious influences interfere with democracy, due process, reason and scientific inquiry. The inalienable domains of human biology and procreation should be regarded no differently than the social and political arenas. Religious bioethics is full of inherent problems and inconsistencies. It's time to dismiss it and acknowledge the efficacy and validity of real and accountable secular bioethics. In biology as in politics, citizens have the right to be free *from* the pressures of organized religion.

1. The name of the Canadian legislation that outlaws therapeutic cloning, etc.

Influenced by Theology

Leon Kass [then chairman of the President's Council of Bioethics], who is fully aware of the negative implications of chairing a religiously biased President's Council on Bioethics, has adamantly declared his brand of ethics to be untainted by theology. On closer inspection, however, his claim is as disingenuous as it is false.

Kass has vigorously studied the Torah [Jewish law] and has written extensively about the Bible, including his book on Genesis, *The Beginning of Wisdom*. He adheres to a conservative form of Judaism, attends synagogue and fasts on Yom Kippur. As Kass himself half-jokingly concedes, "I suffer from a late-onset, probably lethal, rabbinic gene which has gradually expressed itself, and it has taken me over." Further, says Kass, "I've come to treasure the biblical strand of our Western tradition more than the strand that flows from Athens."

So it's no surprise that his particular approach to bioethics betrays an adherence to long-standing Abrahamic [biblical] injunctions against meddling with the human body and reproductive processes. Kass's "wisdom of repugnance" ethics asks us to evaluate issues simply based on how we *feel* about them. "In crucial cases," says Kass, "repugnance is the emotional expression of deep wisdom, beyond reason's power fully to articulate it." According to Kass, those things we find offensive, grotesque, revolting and repulsive are illegitimate and immoral for inexpressible reasons and regardless of what our logic tells us.

The Yuck Factor

This so-called "yuck factor" ethics betrays its religious roots, what sociologist Emile Durkheim described as the religious fixation on the profane and sacred. "All known religious beliefs," wrote Durkheim, "whether simple or complex, present one common characteristic: they presuppose a classification of all the things, real and ideal, of which men think, into two classes or opposed groups, generally designated by two distinct terms which are translated well enough by [the] words *profane* and *sacred*."

Dividing the world into two domains is a tendency that runs rampant in the Abrahamic religious traditions. It is a tradition that insists on the presence of good and evil, simplistic black and white arguments, good guys and bad guys, piety and sin, the natural and the unnatural and, of course, moral meaning in the delineation of those things we find appealing and those things we find yucky.

Elizabeth Blackburn, one of two bioethicists recently removed from the President's Council, has some harsh words for Kass and his yuck factor ethics. "[Kass has] questioned modern medical and biomedical science and taken the stance of a 'moral philosopher,' often invoking a 'wisdom of repugnance'—in other words, rejecting science, such as research involving embryonic stem cells, because it feels wrong to him. I remain convinced that this type of visceral reaction should launch, rather than end, debate."

Blackburn is right. But we can trace the "wisdom of repugnance" beyond a single person. At the heart of his argument, and in true arrogant ultraconservative fashion, what Kass is really proclaiming is that the current cultural norm, or more specifically, the norm that has been established by long-standing religious traditions in the West, is the only true gauge to help us determine what is moral or immoral. And because scientists have a nasty habit of undermining antiquated religious beliefs, and by implication cultural norms, it is most certainly in the best interest of religious conservatives to interfere with scientific advancement to keep the veils of ignorance high and the taboos firmly rooted.

Moral Absolutism

Uninterested in reevaluating ethics and morality in the face of scientific progress, religious conservatives tend to defer to

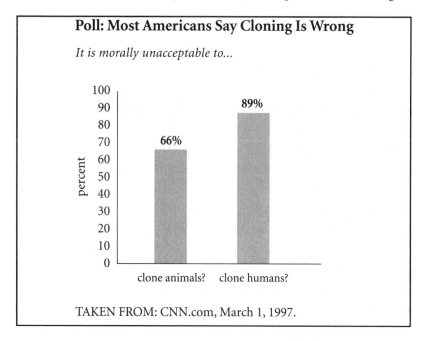

Poll: Most Americans Say Cloning Is Wrong

It is morally unacceptable to...

TAKEN FROM: CNN.com, March 1, 1997.

scripture for moral and existential authority. The Bible is treated as a portal into everything we need to know about anything—end of discussion.

Thus, ethical guidelines that arise from scripture tend to take on the form of absolutism. Since God has supposedly endowed us with the ultimate moral rulebook, religious adherents argue that a fixed and unassailable universal ethics can and should be applied to all people and at all times. In my mind, there is very little that separates this type of reasoning—this moral absolutism—from ideology.

Some might find it comforting to think that we have the answers to everything—especially the answers to deep and complex moral questions—but we don't. By necessity, therefore, what we require is a more sensible approach to formulating our ethics. This is where a relativistic or normative methodology comes in, leading to what is known as situational ethics, as formulated by such thinkers as Joseph Fletcher. Religious followers tend to have fits over this notion, incredulous to the idea that moral values are editable over time or specific to a situation.

Evolving Ethics Needed

However, since the extent of our knowledge at any given point in history is partial at best, we have to continually take stock of what we know about the human condition and add to an evolving and improving set of ethical standards. And while the religious are unwilling to accept this, different social environments—whether those differences arise from social or technological differences—will require different ethics.

Take life support systems for example. The prolongation of life by technological means is leading to some interesting dilemmas in how we treat and define death. We currently declare someone to be dead when their heart stops. But what if someone is completely brain dead and on life support? They are alive in the sense that their body is functioning, but for all intents and purposes, there's nobody home.

Technologies are forcing us to redefine and rethink previously established conventions and practices. Is it right to leave someone who is clearly dead—and permanently so—hooked up to a machine? Christians in particular have no difficulty answering this one, defaulting to scripture and speaking of the "sanctity" of life. Yet the prescientific, . . . authors of the Bible (assuming, of course, that God didn't write it) were never in a position where they had to distinguish between a fully conscious individual and a carcass with a beating heart. Consequently, Christian adherents are following an antiquated version of personhood. And while once reasonable and even helpful, many such religious beliefs are of little value today.

Indeed, as our insight expands due to scientific progress, so too do our ethical sensibilities. What we considered harmful yesterday does not necessarily appear so today; what we consider harmful today, may not seem so tomorrow.

Interracial marriages, for example, were not too long ago considered a repugnant and dangerous social experiment, but very few today would argue today that they are immoral or risky. It's a non-issue. . . .

Similarly, today we are coping with the prospect of same-sex marriages. I predict that in a few decades from now—if not sooner—we will have the same kind of nonchalant attitude to gay and lesbian couples that we currently have to interracial couples.

And I don't use this analogy lightly. Apropos of this discussion, a strong argument can be made that much of our racial and sexual inhibitions were induced by religious mores. Deep Christian values, often mutating into secularized offshoots, permeate our society to this very day. In the past, Christianity in particular has played no small part in the perpetuation of not just racism and anti-homosexual bigotry (including heterocentrism and the insistence on monogamy), but has also contributed to misogyny, sexual repression and the ongoing struggle against biotechnology in general and reproductive freedoms in particular.

Harmful Stands

Religious interference with reproductive practices is particularly problematic, often leading to considerable harm. [In 2003,] the Catholic Church, in a move that I can only describe as pure evil (if I may be allowed to use such a term), declared that condoms do not halt the spread of AIDS because they have tiny holes in them through which HIV can pass. The statement put literally millions of followers at risk.

And in another example of religious meddling, in the US, thanks to the efforts of President Bush and his fourth-century stance on reproductive rights, some women who are about to undergo abortions are being terrorized by clinicians who force them to watch gruesome videos depicting bloody fetuses.

In addition to being flawed, prejudicial and harmful, the Abrahamic ethic also tends to be contradictory, inconsistent and sometimes just plain nonsensical.

As an example, while supposedly upholding the principle of the sanctity of life at all costs, a number of bioconservatives—Kass included—have contradictorily railed against the prospect of life extension technologies. Apparently all life is equal, but some life is less equal than others.

And because religious ethicists believe that personhood begins at conception, it has been argued that work in embryonic stem cells and therapeutic cloning is unethical. But as *Reason*'s [columnist] Ronald Bailey has pointed out, this line of reasoning can lead to some rather bizarre conclusions, including the notion that every cell in the human body should be considered inviolable because, given the right circumstances, every cell could conceivably become a full-grown human being.

It's this kind of alternate reality that religiously influenced bioconservatives tend to operate in, one in which a blastocyst—a microscopic clump of 150 cells—is actually considered not just a person, but a person with equal rights to someone who is fully sentient.

And thus, liberals and social progressives in both Canada and the US march onward in their attempt to derail those who insist on using unfair, dangerous and illogical methodologies. In fact, many of today's reformers and activists—those people who tend to reject absolutist religious ethics—are busy cleaning up the mess of the Christian legacy in the West.

Periodical Bibliography

The following articles have been selected to supplement the diverse views presented in this chapter.

Lori Andrews	"Reproductive Technology Comes of Age," *Whittier Law Review*, vol. 21, 1999.
Keith Betteridge	"Enigmas and Variations Among Mammalian Embryos," *Reproduction of Domestic Animals*, February 2001.
Courier Mail (Queensland, Australia)	"Frozen Embryos Have No Right to Life, Judge Rules," November 16, 2006. www.news.com.au/couriermail/story/0,23739,20767065-401,00.html.
Robert G. Edwards	"Ethical and Moral Issues of In Vitro Fertilization: Introduction; The Scientific Basis of Ethics," *Annals of the New York Academy of Sciences*, vol. 442, 1985.
Ethics Committee of the American Society for Reproductive Medicine	"Access to Fertility Treatment by Gays, Lesbians, and Unmarried Persons," *Fertility and Sterility*, November 2006. www.asrm.org/Media/Ethics/fertility_gaylesunmarried.pdf.
H.J. Leese, I. Donnay, and J.G. Thompson	"Human Assisted Conception: A Cautionary Tale. Lessons from Domestic Animals," *Human Reproduction*, December 1998.
Sally Sheldon	"Stored Embryos, Gender Equality and the Meaning of Parenthood," BioNews.org, December 8, 2006. www.bionews.org.uk/commentary.lasso?storyid=3283.
Patrick Steptoe and Robert Edwards	"Birth After the Reimplantation of a Human Embryo," *Lancet*, August 12, 1978.
Christine Stolba	"Overcoming Motherhood: Pushing the Limits of Reproductive Choice," *Policy Review*, January 2003. www.policyreview.org/DEC02/stolba.html.
D.A. Valone	"The Changing Moral Landscape of Human Reproduction: Two Moments in the History of In Vitro Fertilization," *Mount Sinai Journal of Medicine*, May 1998.

CHAPTER 3

Should Limits Be Placed on Current Reproductive Technologies?

Chapter Preface

Some people believe that reproductive technologies should be banned; others believe that people should be free to make use of any available technology. Most fall somewhere in between. For the majority, where to draw the lines of regulation and limitation has proven difficult to determine.

In vitro fertilization (IVF), the process whereby an egg is fertilized by a sperm in a lab dish and then implanted in the womb, has gained wide acceptance, but its corollaries are controversial. In combination with other technologies, IVF allows for preimplantation genetic diagnosis (PGD), sex selection, and the use of donated gametes. All of these have stirred debate, and none is strictly necessary for IVF to proceed (at least for couples who are capable of producing viable gametes).

PGD allows a couple to know whether their embryo carries genes that will likely lead to genetic disorders, such as Tay Sachs disease or Down syndrome. Such diagnoses give couples the option to refuse implantation of a particular embryo so as to avoid giving birth to a disadvantaged child. This technology has come under criticism, however, by advocates for the disabled, who say that it devalues their lives and will lead to a new round of eugenics in which only those deemed fit to live will be allowed to be born. Proponents rejoin that it is the critics who are attempting to set standards for children; they say that parents should be the ones to decide whether to have a child with a special condition.

Sex selection has been practiced in some parts of the world by abortion or infanticide for centuries. Although such practices horrify many people, new technology allows sex selection prior to conception. Since sex is determined by whether an X (female) or Y (male) sperm fertilizes an egg, the key is to sort the sperm in a sample. Tiny differences in X and Y sperm make this possible. Though not absolutely reliable, the technology does make it relatively easy for a couple to choose the sex of their baby. For critics, this raises fears of "gendercide," or massive selection against girls. Already, critics argue, some countries in Asia have large surpluses of boys because of this practice. Such technology will only worsen the problem, they argue. Others contend that this trend is unlikely to spread to Western nations.

Donated sperm or eggs are crucial to the fertility chances of couples whose problem lies in an insufficiency of viable gametes; however, use of donated gametes encounters powerful opposition in society. Various religions consider third-party involvement in reproduction to be counter to divine will. And there are secular arguments on the question as well: Should donors have some parental responsibility? Should children born of donated gametes have the right to the medical history of the donor? Should anonymity be preserved? All of these are hotly contested questions.

Finally, and perhaps most contentiously, there is the question of what to do with all the frozen embryos. During IVF multiple embryos are created and then only the most promising are implanted. IVF is an uncertain process, and numerous attempts are usually required for a successful birth. The remaining embryos are typically put into cryogenic, or deep-freeze, storage. More than four hundred thousand such embryos are believed to be on hold in the United States alone. This troubles many people. Medical researchers want to tap the embryos for stem cells, which they believe can lead to new cures for many now fatal conditions, but they are strongly opposed by those who regard embryos as being equivalent to babies. For such people, embryo adoption is the best course. President George W. Bush has endorsed embryo adoption. To date, however, only a few hundred successful embryo adoptions have taken place. Whether this is a good solution, and, indeed, whether it is a genuine problem, are matters of continuing debate. Critics point out that frozen embryos were rejected by their creators and are often years old by the time others consider adopting them.

The entire field of reproductive technology tends to stir controversy. This is no surprise, since it involves one of the most intimate and important functions of life. It is especially thorny because it involves not only the private decisions of adult couples but also the future of a new human being.

> "[T]he question is how children feel and how they make sense of their identities when their mother or father (or both) is absent from their daily lives."

Some Reproductive Technologies Should Be Suspended

Elizabeth Marquardt

In the following selection Elizabeth Marquardt argues that technologies that use donated sperm or eggs harm children. Children who lack the presence of both biological parents feel deprived of their full identities, she argues. Reproductive technologies that separate a child from one or both biological parents lead to feelings of abandonment and confusion, Marquardt claims. The answer, she avers, is not simply to remove the shield of anonymity from donors; instead, she calls for a five-year moratorium on all such technologies. Elizabeth Marquardt, a scholar at the Institute for American Values, is the author of Between Two Worlds: The Inner Lives of Children of Divorce. *She lives near Chicago with her husband and two children.*

Elizabeth Marquardt, "Revolution in Parenthood: The Emerging Global Clash Between Adult Rights and Children's Needs," Institute for American Values, September 2006. www.americanvalues.org. Reproduced by permission.

As you read, consider the following questions:

1. According to Marquardt, what is the birthright of a child?

2. What legal complication, according to the author, does revealing a donor parent potentially introduce?

3. What is Marquardt's guiding principle for settling the issues?

Children raised without their own married mother and father often have perspectives about their lives that are radically different from how the legal scholars, courts, and would-be parents expected they would feel. For example, studies on the inner lives of children of divorce are showing an enormous downside for children that was never considered in the heady, early days of the no-fault divorce revolution.

To be perfectly clear, the question is *not* whether children love the parents who raise them. Children almost universally and unquestioningly love their parents, whether their parents are married, divorced, single, gay or straight. Rather, the question is how children feel and how they make sense of their identities when their mother or father (or both) is absent from their daily lives.

The first generation of donor-conceived children who are now coming of age form a remarkable case study to explore this question. Most in this first generation were conceived by married heterosexual couples using donor sperm. Anecdotally, many are now speaking out about the powerful impact on children's identity when adults purposefully conceive a child with the clear intention of separating that child from a biological parent. These young people often say they were denied the birthright of being raised by or at least knowing about their biological fathers. They say that this intentional denial profoundly shapes their quest to understand who they are.

Donor-conceived teenagers and adults are forming organizations, are frequently quoted in news articles, and are using the Internet to try to contact their sperm donors and find half-siblings conceived with the same sperm. They hail from the United States, Canada, Australia, Britain, Japan, and elsewhere. Numbers are hard to come by, but estimates are that the number of children now born in the U.S. each year through artificial insemination range from 30,000 to 75,000 and that about 3,000 each year are conceived using donor eggs. While the numbers arguably are small, they are growing, and the stories these young people tell raise questions not only about their own experience but also about the prospects for the next generation of children born of still more complex reproductive technologies.

No Consent Given

Donor-conceived young people point out that the informed consent of the most vulnerable party—the child—is not obtained in reproductive technology procedures that intentionally separate children from one or both of their biological parents. They ask how the state can aid and defend a practice that denies them their birthright to know and be raised by their own parents and that forcibly conceals half of their genetic heritage. Some call themselves "lopsided" or "half adopted." At least one uses the term "kinship slave." Some born of lesbian or gay parents call themselves "queer spawn," although others in the same situation find the term offensive. No studies have been conducted focusing on these young people's long-term emotional experience. Clearly, rigorous long-term studies need to be done. For now, we should listen to their compelling voices.

Narelle Grech, an Australian donor-conceived woman in her early twenties, asks, "How can you create a child with the full knowledge that he or she will not be able to know about their history and themselves?" She wonders what social message the practice of donor conception gives young men: "Will they think it's OK to get a woman or girl pregnant and that it would be OK to walk away from her, because after all, biology doesn't matter?"

A fellow Australian, Joanna Rose, asks why everyone "flips out" when the wrong baby is taken home from the hospital, yet assumes that donor-conceived children are just fine. She argues: "Our need to know and be known by our genetic relatives is as strong and relevant as anyone else's." She writes, movingly, "I believe that the pain of infertility should not be appeased at the expense of the next generation."

The Missing Half

In interviews, donor-conceived young adults often say something like this: My sperm donor is "half of who I am." One young woman known as Claire is believed to be the first donor offspring to benefit from open-identity sperm donation and have the ability to contact her father upon turning 18. She says she wants to meet her donor because she wants to know "what half of me is, what half of me comes from." Eighteen-year-old Zannah Merricks of London, England says, "I want to meet the donor because I want to know the other half of where I'm from." Lindsay Greenawalt, a young woman from Canton, Ohio who is seeking information about her sperm donor, says, "I feel my right to know who I am and where I come from has been taken away from me."

Eve Andrews, a 17-year-old in Texas, plans to ask the California sperm bank that aided in her conception to forward a letter to her donor when she turns 18. "There's a lot of unanswered questions in my life and I guess I want the answers," she explains. By contrast, her 51-year-old mother, interviewed for the same story, says, "As a woman dealing with the prospect of infertility, all you want is that baby.... It never even occurred to me this child might want to find her biological father someday."

One young man, a 31-year-old doctor in Japan, learned that he was conceived by donor sperm when he examined his parents' white blood cell group while studying medicine. "The most painful thing was the fact that my parents didn't tell me

© CartoonStock.com

for 29 years," he said. "Unless I was told by my parents, I couldn't even exercise my right to know my biological origin."

A 14-year-old girl in Pennsylvania wrote to Dear Abby after finding out she was conceived with donor sperm. In just a few sentences she identified some of the enormous identity issues that confront donor-conceived young people and that are now a challenge to our society. She wrote: "It scares me to think I may have brothers or sisters out there, and that he [my father] may not care that I exist." This young teenager, struggling alone with feelings of abandonment, grief, and confusion, poignantly challenged the current legal and social position on this issue: "I don't understand why it's legal to just donate when a child may be born."

Some observers respond to the voices of donor-conceived adults by saying that there is an inherent contradiction in their argument. These observers say that donor-conceived persons who question the practice of donor conception are wishing away their own existence, and that without the use of a sperm or egg donor or surrogate these young people would not be alive. I find this response highly insensitive. All of us, no matter how we arrived here, should be able to share our stories and struggles in an atmosphere of respect and dignity without being told that we are irrationally ignoring the process that gave us life or are failing to show sufficient appreciation for our life.

Revision of Parenthood

At this moment, with virtually no public discussion, the relationship that is most core and vital to children's very survival—that of parenthood—is being fundamentally redrawn through new laws, proposals, and practices affecting marriage, reproduction, and family life, with the state playing an increasingly active role in defining parenthood for broader categories of children.

Given that in some ways the genie is already out of the bottle, it is not entirely clear what actions the state and social leaders should take in the near future. For instance, some nations have moved to ban the practice of anonymous donation of sperm and eggs. This would seem to be a positive development for children—after all, there is a strong argument to be made that children have a right and need to know their origins. Yet greater acceptance of the idea that donor-conceived children have a right to know their origins is also leading to the idea that these children should have the possibility of some kind of *relationship* with their sperm or egg donor (and not just a file of information), or even that the donor should have some kind of legal parental status in the child's life, such as in New Zealand and Australia where commissions have proposed allowing donors to "opt in" as children's third legal parents.

What might the future hold for children with three or more legal parents? We have no idea.

Untraceable Donors

Or, in another example, after Britain passed a law banning donor anonymity there was a purported drastic drop in the number of men willing to donate sperm. The state health service then began an active campaign to recruit sperm and egg donors, no longer just allowing the intentional conception of children who will not know or be raised in relationship with their own biological parents, but very intentionally promoting it. Meanwhile, couples in that nation who wish to conceive have even greater incentive to go abroad to nations or regions that have less regulation—such as Spain, India, Eastern Europe, or elsewhere—to procure sperm or eggs or surrogate wombs, making it even less likely that their child will ever be able to trace their origins or form a relationship with a distant donor abroad.

Again, how will these developments affect children? At the moment we have no real idea. But we certainly do have serious and immediate cause for concern.

For reasons like these, this report does not conclude with the usual list of specific policy recommendations. Rather, this report issues a call to fellow citizens in the United States and Canada and around the world. The call is for all of us to participate in urgently needed conversation and research about the revolution in parenthood and the needs of children.

A Call to Reconsider

This much is clear: When society changes marriage it changes parenthood. The divorce revolution and the rise in single-parent childbearing weakened ties of fathers to their children and introduced a host of players at times called "parents." The use of assisted reproductive technologies by married heterosexual couples—and later by singles and same-sex couples—raised still more uncertainties about the meaning of motherhood and fatherhood and exposed children to new losses the adults never fathomed. The legalization of same-sex marriage, while sometimes seen as a small change affecting just a few people, raises the startling prospect of fundamentally breaking the legal institution of marriage from any ties to biological parenthood. Meanwhile, successes in the same-sex marriage debate have encouraged others who wish fully and completely to break open the two-person understanding of marriage and parenthood.

Here is where we are. In law and culture, the two-natural-parent, mother-father model is falling away, replaced with the idea that children are fine with any one or more adults being called their parents, so long as the appointed parents are nice people. This change is happening incrementally, largely led by self-appointed experts and advocates in a few fields. But it does not have to be this way. Those of us who are concerned can and should take up and lead a debate about the lives of children and the future of parenthood.

As we launch this conversation, a guiding principle could be this: When there is a clash between adult rights and children's needs, the interests of the more vulnerable party—in this case, the children—should take precedence. A great deal of evidence supports the idea that children, on average, do best when raised by their own, married mother and father, with adoption as an important, pro-child, admirable alternative. With regard to some newly visible family forms, such as families headed by gay or lesbian parents or those created using donor sperm, eggs, or surrogacy, we have more to learn about the lasting, inner experience of the children.

A Five-Year Halt

To provide time and space for this conversation and for more research, this report also calls for a moratorium or a "time out" lasting five years. Until we better understand and prioritize the needs of children, no legislatures, courts, or commissions should press forward with recommendations or changes that broadly undermine the normative importance of mothers and fathers in the lives of children, nor should they support intentionally denying unborn children knowledge of and a relationship with their own mother and father. Rather, they should concentrate their energies on rigorous inquiry and active debate about the needs of children and the role of mothers and fathers in their lives.

The well-being of the world's children calls us to act—not years from now but right now. For their sake, for those born and those yet to be born, we must be willing to launch a sometimes uncomfortable but urgent debate about the well-being of children born in an age that is rapidly redefining the meaning of parenthood. Nothing is inevitable. The time to act is now.

> *"To respect the value of embryonic life, it is not unreasonable to insist that every alternative to embryo research be exhausted before . . . destroying even one embryo."*

Some Reproductive Technologies Should Be Allowed to Proceed with Caution

Paul Lauritzen

In the following selection Paul Lauritzen argues that debates over the use of reproductive technology have been too polarizing, largely because of the focus on whether embryos are persons or property. He pushes for expanding the common ground. Liberals and conservatives agree that an embryo is an awesome thing that deserves respect. That position does not automatically lead, Lauritzen argues, to a ban on use of embryos in reproductive technology or research. However, it shifts the burden of justification onto the shoulders of those who want to make use of embryos in a way that might lead to their destruction. Paul Lauritzen is chair of the Department of Religious Studies and director of the Program in Applied Ethics at John Carroll University in Cleveland, Ohio, and the editor of the book Cloning and the Future of Human Embryo Research.

As you read, consider the following questions:

1. How does Lauritzen characterize the official Catholic instruction on reproduction contained in *Donum Vitae*?
2. How does repugnance or disgust figure into the author's idea that we feel awe toward human embryos?
3. What, in Lauritzen's view, should researchers do before destroying an embryo?

From preimplantation genetic diagnosis to stem cell research, scientific interventions in the reproductive process are forcing us to consider the nature of the early embryo and to answer the question: What is the early embryo? Unfortunately, when that question has been asked in debates about embryo research, the answers have typically been framed in terms reminiscent of debates about abortion, where the extreme positions dominate. Either the fetus is a person with a full set of rights, or it is nothing but a clump of cells with little or no moral claim on us at all. In short, the embryo is either a person or it is a kind of property. In my view, when applied to embryo research, neither extreme is plausible, and to advocate either is in fact morally irresponsible. If we are to think and speak truthfully about embryo research, we must repudiate the extremes and find a middle ground.

The Two Extremes

At one end of the spectrum of views on the status of the embryo is the view that, from conception, the embryo is fully a person with all the rights any person has—most notably the right to life. Although magisterial [the Catholic Church's] teaching is not definitive on this point, the common perception and the public posture of Catholic teaching on the status of the embryo accords with this extreme view. We see this, for example, in the Instruction *Donum Vitae*, issued by the Vatican's Congregation for the Doctrine of the Faith [C.D.F.] in 1987, where we read: "The human being is to be respected and treated as a person from the moment of conception; and therefore from the same moment his rights as a person must be recognized, among which in the first place is the inviolable right of every innocent being to life."

The implication of this view of the fetus for Catholic teaching on abortion has long been clear: abortion is an abominable crime. In *Donum Vitae*, however, the C.D.F. draws out the implications of this view of the fetus for embryo research as well. "No objective," the C.D.F. writes, "can in any way justify experimentation on living human embryos or fetuses, whether viable or not, either inside or outside the mother's womb." Indeed, this has been the consistent response of the Catholic Church to every new development in reproductive technology that involves manipulating early embryos. Whether the issue is *in vitro* fertilization (I.V.F.) or embryo freezing, preimplantation genetic diagnosis or embryonic stem cell research, all are wrong—indeed, the suggestion is that all are murderous—because all typically involve the destruction of a living person.

At the other end of the spectrum stands the view that the early embryo is little more than cellular material, which demands little, if anything, of us morally. Although such a view of the fetus is rarely openly admitted, it is, I believe, more pervasive than many liberals would care to admit. Reductionistic views of the fetus are often found, for example, in the writings of those whose moral views are shaped by the law.

Consider the work of the well-known and influential legal scholar John Robertson. Although Robertson would probably dispute the characterization of his view as the extreme one that embryos are merely biological material, the way he frames his discussion of embryo research and the uses of the embryos that he sanctions indicates that his view is extreme. For Robertson, the real question in the debate about embryo research is whether the reproductive freedom that justifies assisted reproduction also justifies embryo research. Thus, in his book, *Children of Choice*, Robertson tells us that the fundamental question is this: "Does procreative liberty entitle people to use their reproductive capacity to produce products or material to serve nonreproductive ends?" Once the question is framed in this way, the only real reason to oppose embryo research is that it may involve a kind of symbolic harm to embryos, and this harm will almost always be outweighed by the potential benefits of embryo research. So where the Catholic Church opposes most non-therapeutic embryo research as profoundly wrong, Robertson endorses most forms of embryo research, because for him the loss of embryonic life is profoundly insignificant.

Extreme Views Miss the Mark

What should we make of these extreme views? Although I cannot here develop the detailed arguments that would demonstrate the inadequacy of the two extreme positions, let me note a general problem for both views. I will then conclude with some comments about how we might make progress on this issue. The problem is that for neither position does the rhetoric match the reality of moral practice. If we took seriously, for example, the rhetoric of many pro-life advocates about embryo research, we ought to be in the streets fighting not merely to restrict such research but to shut down every I.V.F. clinic in the country. To describe I.V.F. and embryo research as murdering children, as former Republican presidential candidate Gary Bauer has done, is implicitly to issue a call for tireless social action to halt the carnage. Yet no such effort has been made to halt I.V.F., nor is there likely to be one; because most people recognize that however morally problematic destroying early embryos is, it is not murder.

Helping Patients, Respecting Embryos

"Few would likely argue that suffering patients do not deserve help; however, these arguments do not address how respect is shown for the embryo while the utilitarian calculus or the moral imperative is fulfilled. To meet the mandate for respect, the embryos used in research must be spare embryos that would otherwise be discarded. Often, the number of embryos created in the process of fertility treatments exceeds the number of embryos needed to achieve the couple's reproductive goals. In that situation, there are three possible scenarios for dealing with the leftover embryos: donating or adopting the embryo for transfer into a donee's uterus for purposes of gestation, permanently storing the embryo, or abandoning the embryo by discarding it or donating it for research. . . . Potential donors should not be asked to provide the embryo for research purposes until they have independently decided that discarding the embryo is their preferred option; that is, the donors should have decided that the embryo will not be adopted or permanently stored before they consider donating the embryo for research. Once this limitation on the timing of the decision to donate an embryo for research is incorporated, the three above-mentioned scenarios for dealing with embryos remain. Each of these scenarios demonstrates respect for the embryo as a symbol of life in a different way."

Heather Johnson Kukla, Georgetown Law Journal, *January 2002.*

At the same time, however, the view that the early embryo is merely cellular material is equally implausible. In recent years, Leon Kass [former chairman of the President's Council on Bioethics] has spoken of the "wisdom of repugnance" in relation to cloning, but over 20 years ago Kass demonstrated this point dramatically in considering the status of the early embryo. If you are inclined to think that the embryo is just so much biological stuff, he said, try to imagine your reaction to the prospect of eating the blastocyst as a kind of human caviar (*Toward a More Natural Science*). The revulsion we feel at this prospect should be enough to show us that the embryo, even the earliest embryo, is not nothing. It is life, indeed human life, which deserves respect.

That the rhetoric of those who dismiss the embryo's status as insignificant does not match their moral practice is suggested by the fact that even so staunch a supporter of procreative liberty as John Robertson does not believe that anything goes. Although, as we saw, Robertson talks about the creation of "products or material," and although the chapter in which he uses such language is entitled "Farming the Uterus," Robertson does not endorse all forms of embryo research. Indeed, even Robertson's rhetoric is sometimes curbed, as when he talks about the embryo deserving respect.

An Alternative Approach

If it is a mistake to think of the early embryo either as a person or merely as a clump of cells, how should we think of the embryo? Let me take a suggestion from the legal philosopher Ronald Dworkin. In his book *Life's Dominion*, Dworkin has argued that the problem with debates about abortion is that they have mostly been conducted as if the fundamental question is whether the fetus or embryo is a person. Framing the debate in this way inevitably leads to the sort of extreme positions that we have just noted. Instead of arguing about whether the fetus is a person—a debate that is polarizing precisely because it invites a yes-or-no answer—Dworkin notes that the actions of both camps suggest common ground. "The truth," Dworkin writes, "is that liberal opinion, like the conservative view, presupposes that human life has intrinsic moral significance, so that it is in principle wrong to terminate a life even when no one's interests are at stake."

My suggestion, then, is that we abandon the rhetoric that gives us the choice: either person or property. Instead, let us highlight the awe and reverence that nearly everyone feels at the miracle of life. If the embryo is not a person, it is certainly a developing form of human life and as such deserves respect. It seems to me that Leon Kass got it right all those years ago when he wrote: "In the blastocyst, even in the zygote, we face a mysterious and awesome power, a power governed by an immanent plan that may produce an indisputably and fully human being. It deserves our respect not because it has rights or claims to sentience but because of what it is, now and prospectively."

Such a view of the embryo may not seem far removed from Catholic teaching; certainly it is closer to church teaching than the view of someone like John Robertson. Yet to speak of the sanctity of human life, even the absolute obligation of respecting the life of the early embryo, is importantly different from speaking of an absolute obligation not to conduct embryo research. Such a view will not sanction talk of categorical evil or of murder or of killing children when discussing embryo research. Instead, celebrating the wonder that is human life, from its earliest moments to its last, will lead to a moral presumption against embryo research.

Burden of Proof

Concretely, this means that the burden of proof rests on those who wish to conduct such research. It also means that we need to develop criteria by which we will determine if the burden has been met. Articulating and defending appropriate criteria is beyond the scope of this essay. Nevertheless, let me in closing suggest three possible tests. Borrowing from just war theory, we might insist that there be a just cause for any proposed research involving the embryo and that such research be both proportionate and of last resort. If we were to develop these three conditions carefully, I suspect that we would find that many proposed forms of embryo research fail the test.

Consider, for example, the case of embryonic stem cell research in light of the condition of last resort. In a letter to the National Institutes of Health Office of Science Policy, the general secretary for the N.C.C.B./U.S.C.C. [National Council of Catholic Bishops/United States Catholic Conference], the then Msgr. Dennis Schnurr, pointed out on behalf of the American bishops that the promising work being done on adult stem cells eliminates the need for embryonic stem cell research. "The existence of such startling new alternatives [as adult stem research], which may be much more amenable to clinical use and do not require any destruction of human life," he wrote, "poses a significant new issue for ethics and public policy"(www.nccbuscc.org/prolife/issues/bioethic/comments.htm). Although Bishop Schnurr does not name the issue as that of last resort, his point is surely that advocates of embryonic stem cell research have not demonstrated that embryo research is the only possible avenue to the many promised clinical benefits of stem cell research. Indeed, they have not even tried. Yet, if we are to respect the value of embryonic life, it is not unreasonable to insist that every alternative to embryo research be exhausted before we consider the possibility of destroying even one embryo.

"Is there any valid justification for criminalizing social sex selection . . . for, say, helping the parents of three boys to finally conceive a girl? I don't think so."

Sex Selection Technologies Should Be Left to Parental Choice

Edgar Dahl

In the viewpoint that follows, bioethicist Edgar Dahl dismisses calls to ban sex selection. He notes that fears about negative consequences have led several countries to ban technologies that permit prospective parents to choose the sex of their child; however, Dahl cites polling data that suggest that few people in Western countries have a strong preference for one sex or the other. Noting that moral distinctions can be drawn, he also rejects the argument that allowing sex selection would lead to "designer babies." Since no convincing case against sex selection can be made, Dahl argues, the practice should be allowed. Edgar Dahl is a bioethicist on the faculty of the University of Giessen, Germany. He is a member of the International Association of Bioethics and the German Academy for Ethics in Medicine.

Edgar Dahl, "Boy or Girl: Should Parents Be Allowed to Choose the Sex of Their Children?" Cardiff Centre for Ethics Law & Society, February 2005. www.ccels.cf.ac.uk. © 2005 Ashgate Publishing Ltd. Reproduced by permission.

As you read, consider the following questions:

1. How does MicroSort technology facilitate sex selection, according to Dahl?

2. What is the highest percentage of people polled who prefer to have more boys than girls, as reported by the author?

3. How, according to Dahl, can society permit sex selection but prevent selection for intelligence?

For centuries, couples have been trying to influence the sex of their children by myriads of dubious tricks. Italian men were biting their wife's left ear during intercourse to beget a daughter and their right ear to sire a son. Swedish men were hanging their pants on the left bedpost to father a girl and on the right one to father a boy. German woodcutters were taking an axe to bed and then chanted: "Ruck, ruck, roy, you shall have a boy!" or "Ruck, ruck, raid, you shall have a maid!" Needless to say, all these old wives' tales turned out to be a forlorn hope.

Sex selection is now a reality. Thanks to MicroSort, a new technology currently being tested in an FDA [Food and Drug Administration] approved clinical trial, parents will soon be able to choose the sex of their children prior to conception. MicroSort allows [separating] the sperm that produce a boy from the sperm that produce a girl. The separated sperm can then be used for artificial insemination. If a couple would like to have a son, the woman will be inseminated with male-producing sperm only; if a couple would like to have a daughter, the woman will be inseminated with female-producing sperm only. Given that not every attempt of artificial insemination results in a pregnancy, couples will have to undergo an average of three to five cycles of insemination. Each attempt will cost about 1,250 British Pounds [about $2,400]. All expenses incurred must be covered by the couple undergoing treatment.

It will probably take another two or three years until the safety and efficacy of MicroSort has been properly established. Given the current results ... there is virtually no doubt that the technology will get the approval of the US Food and Drug Administration. If so, Fertility Centers around the globe may apply for a sublicence to use MicroSort and to offer their own service for preconception sex selection.

Bans in Europe

To prevent British fertility specialists from offering MicroSort for social reasons, the Human Fertilisation and Embryology Authority (HFEA) recently advised the government of the United Kingdom to enact a law prohibiting sex selection for any but the most serious of medical reasons. Great Britain will not be the first Western society outlawing non-medical sex selection. In 1990, Germany passed its notorious Embryo Protection Act making social sex selection a criminal offence punishable by one year of imprisonment. In the Australian state of Victoria, the sentence is even harsher. According to section 50 of the Infertility Treatment Act of 1995 doctors performing sex selection for non-medical reasons face up to two years imprisonment.

Is there any valid justification for criminalizing social sex selection and for sentencing a doctor to jail for, say, helping the parents of three boys to finally conceive a girl? I don't think so—at least not in a Western liberal democracy. . . .

Each citizen should have the right to live his life as he chooses so long as he does not infringe upon the rights of others. The state may interfere with the free choices of its citizens only to prevent serious harm to others.

Liberty First

The presumption in favour of liberty has at least three important implications. Firstly, the burden of proof is always on those who opt for a legal prohibition of a particular action. It

How to Choose a Baby's Sex

"This is a very general idea of the MicroSort process. A semen sample is separated in the MicroSort sperm sorter using a technique called flow cytometry. An XSort results in mostly girl-producing X sperm, or a YSort results in mostly boy-producing Y sperm. The sorted sample is then used to get pregnant, either by artificial insemination (IUI) or in-vitro fertilization (IVF)."

"MicroSort Sperm Sorting," In-Gender.com.
www.in-gender.com/gender-selection/MicroSort/.

is they who must show that the action in question is going to harm others. Secondly, the evidence for the harm to occur has to be clear and persuasive. It must not be based upon highly speculative sociological or psychological assumptions. And thirdly, the mere fact that an action may be seen by some as contrary to their moral or religious beliefs does not suffice for a legal prohibition. The domain of the law is not the enforcement of morality, but the prevention of harm to others.

With this in mind, let us turn to some of the most common objections to sex selection and see whether they provide a rational basis for outlawing it.

A constantly recurring objection to sex selection is that choosing the sex of our children is to 'play God'. This religious objection has been made to all kinds of medical innovations. For example, using chloroform to relieve the pain of childbirth was considered contrary to the will of God as it avoided the 'primeval curse on woman'. Similarly, the use of inoculations was opposed with sermons preaching that diseases are 'sent by Providence' for the punishment of sin and it is wrong of man to escape from such divine retribution. Since even fundamentalist Christians ceased to regard the alleviation of pain and the curing of diseases as morally impermissible, it is hard to take this objection seriously. What was once seen as 'playing God' is now seen as acceptable medical practice. More importantly, the objection that sex selection is a violation of 'God's Law' is an explicit religious claim. As Western liberal democracies are based on a strict separation of state and church, no government is entitled to pass a law to enforce compliance with a specific religion. People who consider the option of sex selection as contrary to their religious belief are free to refrain from it, but they are not permitted to use the coercive power of the law to impose their theology upon all those who do not share their religious world view.

Unnatural Is Not Immoral

Some are opposed to sex selection because they have the feeling it is somehow 'unnatural'. Like the objection that choosing the sex of our children is playing God, the claim that sex selection is not natural most often expresses an intuitive reaction rather than a clearly reasoned moral response. That a particular human action is unnatural does in no way imply that it is morally wrong. To transplant a heart to save a human life is certainly unnatural, but is it for that reason immoral? Surely not! Thus, if we have to decide whether an action is morally right or wrong we cannot settle the issue by asking whether it is natural or unnatural.

A more serious objection to sex selection is based on the claim that medical procedures ought to be employed for medical purposes only. Flow cytometric sperm separation, it is argued, is a medical technology designed to enable couples who are at risk of transmitting a severe sex-linked genetic disorder to have a healthy child. In the absence of a known risk to transmit a serious X-linked disease, there is simply no valid justification for employing flow cytometric sperm separation. This is a familiar objection in debates over novel applications of genetic and reproductive technologies. However, as familiar as it may be, it is certainly not a persuasive one. We have already become accustomed to a medical system in which physicians often provide services that have no direct medical benefit but that do have great personal value for the individuals seeking it. Given the acceptance of breast enlargements, hair replacements, ultrasound assisted liposuctions and other forms of cosmetic surgery, one cannot, without calling that system into question, condemn a practice merely because it uses a medical procedure for lifestyle or child-rearing choices.

A related objection insists that offering a service for social sex selection constitutes an inappropriate use of limited medical resources. Again, if offering face-lifts is not considered to be a misallocation of scarce medical resources, it is hard to see how offering sex selection can be considered to be a misallocation of scarce medical resources. Moreover, by implying that every time a patient gets a nose-job another patient misses out on a bypass, this objection betrays a severely distorted conception of economics. If at all, this argument may apply to a state-run socialist economy based on a Five-Year Plan, but certainly not to a private-run capitalist economy based on a free market. Just like a chef opening up a fancy restaurant offering French cuisine does not deprive us of our daily bread, so a doctor opening up a fertility center offering sex selection does not deprive us of our basic health care. Provided their businesses are set up privately and their services are paid for privately, they don't take away from anyone.

Gender Imbalance

Perhaps the most powerful objection to sex selection is that it may distort the natural sex ratio and lead to a severe imbalance of the sexes, as has occurred in countries such as India, China, and Korea. A surplus of men and a shortage of women, some sociologists have predicted, will invariably cause an enormous rise in enforced celibacy, homosexuality, polyandry, prostitution, molestation, rape and other sex-related crimes.

However, whether or not a drastic distortion of the natural sex ratio poses a real threat to Western societies is, of course, an empirical question that cannot be answered by mere intuition, but only by scientific evidence. For a severe sex ratio distortion to occur, at least two conditions have to be met. First, there must be a significant preference for children of a particular sex, and second there must be a considerable demand for sex selection services. The available empirical evidence suggests that neither condition is met in Western societies. According to representative social surveys conducted in Germany, the United Kingdom and the United States, the overwhelming majority of couples desires to have an equal number of boys and girls—usually two children, one boy and one girl.

For instance, when asked "If given a choice, would you like to have only boys, only girls, more boys than girls, more girls than boys, or an equal number of boys and girls?", 1% of Germans stated that they prefer to have only boys, 1% only girls, 4% more boys than girls, 3% more girls than boys, 30% as many boys as girls, and 58% said they had no preference whatsoever. Similarly, in the UK 3% preferred only boys, 2% only girls, 6% more boys than girls, 4% more girls than boys, 68% an equal number of boys and girls, and 16% did not care about the sex of their future children. And, finally, in the US 5% preferred only boys, 4% only girls, 7% more boys than girls, 6% more girls than boys, 50% the same number of boys and girls, and 27% simply did not mind the sex of their offsping.

As we know all too well, there is often a yawning gap between what people say and what they actually do. However, demographic research does indeed confirm the stated preference for a so-called "gender balanced family". Couples with two boys and couples with two girls are more likely to have a third child than couples with one boy and one girl—suggesting that parents with children of both sexes are much more content with their family composition. This distinct trend towards a balanced family has not only been observed in Germany, the UK and the US, but also in Canada, Italy, Spain, Sweden, Belgium, Austria, Switzerland and The Netherlands.

Family Balancing

Even more instructive than social surveys and demographic research are data collected by so-called Gender Clinics. Worldwide, there are already about 75 Fertility Centers that offer some method of sperm sorting followed by artificial insemination. According to the leading Gender Clinic, the MicroSort Unit of the Genetics & IVF Institute in Fairfax, Virginia, well over 90 percent of couples seeking social sex selection are parents who already have two or three children of the same sex and long to have just one more child of the opposite sex.

In conclusion, the widespread fear of a sex ratio distortion seems to be unjustified. The existing empirical evidence suggests that a readily available service for preconception sex selection will have only a negligible societal impact and is highly unlikely to cause a severe imbalance of the sexes in Western societies.

Although the threat of a sex ratio distortion is potentially the most troubling problem, it is also a problem that is easily resolved—namely by limiting the service for sex selection to the purpose of "family balancing". If access to sex selection were restricted to parents having at least two children of the same sex, then helping them to have a child of the opposite sex would, if at all, only marginally alter the balance of the sexes.

Another frequently advanced objection claims that sex selection is "inherently sexist". For example, the feminist philosopher Tabitha Powledge argues that, "we should not choose the sexes of our children because to do so is one of the most stupendously sexist acts in which it is possible to engage. It is the original sexist sin." Sex selection, she continues, is deeply wrong because it makes "the most basic judgment about the worth of a human being rest first and foremost on its sex." However, this argument is deeply flawed. It is simply false that all people who would like to choose the sex of their children are motivated by the sexist belief that one sex is more valuable than the other. As we have seen, almost all couples seeking sex selection are simply motivated by the desire to have at least one child of each sex. If this desire is based on any beliefs at all, it is based on the quite defensible assumption that raising a girl is different from raising a boy, but certainly not on the belief that one sex is 'superior' to the other.

A further common objection concerns the welfare of children born as a result of sex selection. Thus, it has been argued that sex selected children may be expected to behave in certain gender specific ways and risk to be resented if they fail to do so. Although it cannot be completely ruled out, it is highly unlikely that children conceived after MicroSort are going to suffer from unreasonable parental expectations. Couples seeking sex selection to ensure the birth of a daughter are very well aware that they can expect a girl, not some Julia Roberts; and couples going for a son know perfectly well they can expect a boy, not some Hugh Grant.

Drawing Lines

Last but not least, there is the widely popular objection that sex selection is the first step down a road that will inevitably lead to the creation of "designer babies." Once we allow parents to choose the sex of their children, we will soon find ourselves allowing them to choose their eye colour, their height, or their intelligence. This slippery slope objection calls for three remarks. First, it is not an argument against sex selection, but only against its alleged consequences. Second, and more importantly, it is based on the assumption that we are simply incapable of preventing the alleged consequences from happening. However, this view is utterly untenable. It is perfectly possible to draw a legal line permitting some forms of selection and prohibiting others. Thus, if selection for sex is morally acceptable but selection for, say, intelligence is not, the former can be allowed and the latter not. And third, the slippery slope argument presumes that sliding down the slope is going to have detrimental, if not devastating, social effects. However, in the case of selecting offspring traits this is far from obvious. What is so terrifying about the idea that some parents may be foolish enough to spend their hard-earned money on genetic technologies just to ensure their child will be born with big brown eyes and black curly hair? I am sorry, but I cannot see that this would herald the end of civilization as we know it.

Since it cannot be established that preconception sex selection would cause any serious harm to others, a legal ban is ethically unjustified. However, that sex selection ought not to be prohibited does not preclude regulating its practice. For example, to limit sex selection services to licensed centres subject to monitoring by health authorities seems entirely appropriate. This would not only guarantee high scientific standard and high quality professional care, but it would also enable detailed research on possible demographic consequences and thus allow action if—contrary to expectations—significant imbalances were to develop.

"The preferences of prospective parents are obviously relevant in child-bearing matters, but so [is] the well-being of future children."

Sex Selection Technologies Should Not Be Left to Parental Choice

Marcy Darnovsky

In the following viewpoint Marcy Darnovsky argues that parental choice alone is not enough to justify approval of sex selection technology. She warns that the commercialization of such technology raises concerns that it will fuel sexism and gender stereotypes and possibly pave the way to consumer-driven eugenics. The question, she argues, is not whether parents are satisfied with such a system, but whether the best interests of children are being safeguarded. Marcy Darnovsky is associate executive director of the Center for Genetics and Society. She has taught courses on the politics of science, technology, and the environment at the Hutchins School of Liberal Studies at Sonoma State University in California.

Marcy Darnovsky, "Revisiting Sex Selection," *GeneWatch*, January–February 2004. www.gene-watch.org. Reproduced with permission of *GeneWatch*, printed by the Council for Responsible Genetics.

As you read, consider the following questions:

1. Why does Darnovsky differ with feminists who worry that restricting sex selection would restrict abortion rights?

2. According to the author, what danger for the rest of the world looms if the United States legitimizes sex selection?

3. What does Darnovsky think about the morality of wishing for a child of a particular sex?

In the United States and a few other prosperous, technologically advanced nations, methods of sex selection that are less intrusive or more reliable than older practices are now coming into use. Unlike prenatal testing, these procedures generally are applied either before an embryo is implanted in a woman's body, or before an egg is fertilized. They do not require aborting a fetus of the "wrong" sex.

These pre-pregnancy sex selection methods are being rapidly commercialized—not, as before, with medical claims, but as a means of satisfying parental desires. For the assisted reproduction industry, social sex selection may be a business path toward a vastly expanded market. People who have no infertility or medical problems, but who can afford expensive out-of-pocket procedures, are an enticing new target.

Ads for Gender Choice

For the first time, some fertility clinics are openly advertising sex selection for social reasons. Several times each month, for example, the *New York Times*' Sunday Styles section carries an ad from the Virginia-based Genetics & IVF (in-vitro fertilization) Institute, touting its patented sperm sorting method. Beside a smiling baby, its boldface headline asks, "Do You Want to Choose the Gender of Your Next Baby?"

Recent trends in consumer culture may warm prospective parents to such offers. We have become increasingly accepting of—if not enthusiastic about—"enhancements" of appearance (think face-lifts, collagen and Botox injections, and surgery to reshape women's feet for stiletto heels) and adjustments of behavior (anti-depressants, Viagra, and the like). These drugs and procedures were initially developed for therapeutic uses, but are now being marketed and normalized in disturbing ways. When considering questions of right and wrong, of liberty and justice, it is well to remember that the state is not the only coercive force we encounter.

This constellation of technological, economic, cultural, and ideological developments has revived the issue of sex selection, relatively dormant for more than a decade. The concerns that have always accompanied sex selection debates are being reassessed and updated. These include the prospect that selection could reinforce misogyny, sexism, and gender stereotypes; undermine the well-being of children by treating them as commodities and subjecting them to excessive parental expectations or disappointment; skew sex ratios in local populations; further the commercialization of reproduction; and open the door to a high-tech consumer eugenics.

Feminist Concerns

Sex selection is not a new issue for U.S. feminists. In the 1980s and early 1990s, it was widely discussed and debated, especially by feminist bioethicists. This was the period when choosing a boy or girl was accomplished by undergoing prenatal diagnostic tests to determine the sex of a fetus, and then terminating the pregnancy if the fetus was of the undesired sex.

Ultrasound scanning and amniocentesis, which had been developed during the 1970s to detect, and usually to abort, fetuses with Down's syndrome and other conditions, were on their way to becoming routine in wealthier parts of the world. Soon they were also being openly promoted as tools for enabling sex-selective abortions in South and East Asian countries where the cultural preference for sons is pervasive. Opposition in these countries, especially strong in India, mounted in the early 1980s and remains vibrant today.

Throughout the 1980s and early 1990s, feminists and others in the U.S. who addressed the issue of sex selection were—almost universally—deeply uneasy about it. Not all opposed it equally, but none were enthusiastic or even supportive.

Some, like Helen Bequaert Holmes, pointed out that the deliberate selection of the traits of future generations is a form of eugenics. Many deplored the practice as a symptom of a sexist society, in effect if not always in intent. In a book-length treatment of these concerns, published in 1985, philosopher Mary Anne Warren asked whether the practice should be considered an aspect of what she dubbed 'gendercide'—"no less a moral atrocity than genocide"—and published an entire book on the topic in 1985.

But there was also broad consensus among feminists that any effort to limit sex-selective abortions, especially in the U.S., would threaten reproductive rights. Warren, despite her misgivings, argued that choosing the sex of one's child was sexist only if its intent or consequence was discrimination against women. She concluded that "there is great danger that the legal prohibition of sex selection would endanger other aspects of women's reproductive freedom," and considered even moral suasion against the practice to be unwarranted and counterproductive.

By the mid-1990s, the discussion had reached an impasse. No one liked sex selection, but few were willing to actively oppose it. Sex selection largely faded as an issue of concern for U.S. feminists, especially outside the circles of an increasingly professionalized bioethics discourse.

Libertarian Claims

The new technologies of sex selection (and, perhaps, their potential profits) have prompted some bioethicists to argue in favor of allowing parents to choose their offspring's sex. As in past debates on other assisted reproductive procedures, they frame their advocacy in terms of "choice," "liberty," and "rights." John Robertson, a lawyer and bioethicist close to the fertility industry, is one of the leading proponents of this approach. In a lead article of the Winter 2001 issue of *American Journal of Bioethics*, Robertson wrote, "The risk that exercising rights of procreative liberty would hurt offspring or women—or contribute to sexism generally—is too speculative and uncertain to justify infringement of those rights."

Robertson's claims are based on a world view that gives great weight to individual preferences and liberties, and little to social justice and the common good. As political scientist Diane Paul writes in a commentary on Robertson's recent defense of "preconception gender selection," "If you begin with libertarian premises, you will inevitably end up having to accept uses of reprogenetic technology that are even more worrisome" than sex selection.

Definitions of procreative liberty like Robertson's are expansive—indeed, they often seem limitless. . . .

High-Tech Eugenics

When Mary Anne Warren considered sex selection in 1985, she summarily dismissed concerns of its contribution to a new eugenics as "implausible" on the grounds that "[t]here is at present no highly powerful interest group which is committed to the development and use of immoral forms of human genetic engineering."

However, less than two decades later, a disturbing number of highly powerful figures are in fact committed to the development and use of a form of human genetic engineering that huge majorities here and abroad consider immoral—inheritable genetic modification, or manipulating the genes passed on to our children. These scientists, bioethicists, biotech entre-

Sex Bias in America's Indian Community

"The real issue is not necessarily sex selection per se, but what sex selection signifies—the unequal status of women. While many couples say they need to have a son since they already have daughters, many do not know how to answer me when I ask if they would seek a daughter if they had only sons. Technology or physicians alone are not at the root of the problem. The use of technology and marketing of sex selection exist because of the preference for a male child. Technological advancement undoubtedly increases the pressure to use technology in order to have a boy. One woman told me, 'Now that all these methods exist, if I don't use them, my in-laws will harass me.' While I understand the role that technology plays in making this issue worse, ultimately it is the deep-seated preference for boys that we must question and challenge. For instance, why is it that some couples believe they have 'too many daughters,' but we rarely hear complaints about 'too many sons'?"

Sunita Puri, India Currents, *March 17, 2006.*

preneurs, and libertarians are actively advocating a new market-based, high-tech eugenics.

Princeton University molecular biologist Lee Silver, for example, positively anticipates the emergence of genetic castes and human sub-species. "[T]he GenRich class and the Natural class will become ... entirely separate species," he writes, "with no ability to cross-breed, and with as much romantic interest in each other as a current human would have for a chimpanzee." Nobel laureate James Watson promotes redesigning the genes of our children with statements such as, "People say it would be terrible if we made all girls pretty. I think it would be great."

Silver's and Watson's remarks (and all too many similar ones) refer to technologies that are being used routinely in lab animals, but have not been applied to human beings. However, pre-implantation genetic diagnosis (PGD), the most common new sex selection method, is very much related to these technologies. It was introduced in 1990 as a way to identify and discard embryos affected by serious genetic conditions, and thus prevent the birth of children with particular traits. Though PGD is touted as a medical tool, disability advocates have pointed out that many people who have the conditions it targets live full and satisfying lives. PGD, they say, is already a eugenic technology....

Suppression of Girls

In 1992, Nobel Prize–winning economist Amartya Sen estimated the number of "missing women" worldwide, lost to neglect, infanticide, and sex-specific abortions, at one hundred million. Similarly shocking figures were confirmed by others.

Many in the global North are distressed by the pervasiveness and persistence of sex-selective abortions in South and East Asia, and believe bans on sex selection procedures may be warranted there. At the same time, some of these people believe sex selection in countries without strong traditions of son preference may not be so bad.

This double standard rests on shaky grounds. The increased use and acceptance of sex selection in the U.S. would legitimize its practice in other countries, while undermining opposition by human rights and women's rights groups there. Even *Fortune* [magazine] recognized this dynamic. "It is hard to overstate the outrage and indignation that MicroSort [a sperm-sorting method] prompts in people who spend their lives trying to improve women's lot overseas," it noted in 2001.

In addition, there are also large numbers of South Asians living in European and North American countries, and sex selection ads in *India Abroad* and the North American edition of *Indian Express* have specifically targeted them. South Asian feminists in these communities fear that sex selection could take new hold among immigrants who retain a preference for sons. They decry the numerous ways it reinforces and exacerbates misogyny, including violence against women who fail to give birth to boys. If these practices are unacceptable—indeed, often illegal—in South Asia (and elsewhere), should they be allowed among Asian communities in the West? . . .

That North Americans may not use new technologies to produce huge numbers of "extra" boys does not, however, mean that sex selection and sexism are unrelated. One study, by Roberta Steinbacher at Cleveland State University, found that 81% of women and 94% of men who say they would use sex selection would want their firstborn to be a boy. Steinbacher notes that the research literature on birth order is clear: firstborns are more aggressive and higher-achieving than their siblings. "We'll be creating a nation of little sisters," she says.

Observers of sex selection point to another discriminatory impact: its potential for reinforcing gender stereotyping. Parents who invest large amounts of money and effort in order to "get a girl" are likely to have a particular kind of girl in mind. As a mother of one of the first MicroSort babies recalled, "I wanted to have someone to play Barbies with and to go shopping with; I wanted the little girl with long hair and pink fingernails."

There are many reasons people may wish for a daughter instead of a son, or a boy rather than a girl. In a sympathetic account, *New York Times* reporter and feminist Lisa Belkin described some of the motivations of U.S. women who are "going for the girl."

"They speak of Barbies and ballet and butterfly barrettes," she writes, but "they also describe the desire to rear strong young women. Some want to re-create their relationships with their own mothers; a few want to do better by their daughters than their mothers did by them. They want their sons to have sisters, so that they learn to respect women. They want their husbands to have little girls. But many of them want a daughter simply because they always thought they would have one."

Children's Interests Count

Compelling though some of these longings may be, sex selection cannot be completely understood or appropriately confronted by evaluating the rightness or wrongness of parental desires. The preferences of prospective parents are obviously relevant in child-bearing matters, but so are the well-being of future children and the social consequences of technologies—especially those that are already being aggressively marketed.

Wishing for a girl, or for a boy, is cause for neither shame nor condemnation. But as legal scholar Dorothy Roberts points out, it is important to "scrutinize the legal and political context which helps to both create and give meaning to individuals' motivations."

If wishes, choices, and preferences are to be appropriately balanced with social justice and the common good, they cannot be unthinkingly transformed into protected liberties, much less codified rights.

"Whether a woman is 60 or 16, she, and not some committee, is best placed to make the choice about the kind of family she wants to have."

Older Women Should Be Allowed to Use Reproductive Technologies to Become Mothers

Jennie Bristow

In the following viewpoint Jennie Bristow dismisses all the fuss about older mothers achieving pregnancy through reproductive technology. The decision to become a mother is essentially a private one, whatever the age of the prospective parent, she argues. Moreover, there is no essential difference between conceiving naturally and becoming pregnant with the assistance of reproductive technology, she claims. The only distressing difference, Bristow notes, is that an older woman making use of in vitro fertilization (IVF) is liable to find herself criticized in the media. Jennie Bristow is a member of a libertarian Marxist group that opposes restrictions on business, science, and biotechnology. She is also an editor of the online forum Spiked.

Jennie Bristow, "What's Wrong with the World's Oldest Mum?" *Spiked*, January 18, 2005. Copyright © *Spiked* 2000–2005. All rights reserved. Reproduced by permission.

As you read, consider the following questions:

1. Why does Bristow think it is hypocritical to object to older women using IVF as unnatural?

2. Why does the author object to "suitability tests" for prospective IVF users?

3. Who, according to Bristow, is best placed to make decisions about mothering?

'First baby for the world's oldest mother (and she's single).' In this *Daily Mail* [London] headline, the parentheses say it all. If it wasn't bad enough that a 66-year-old Romanian woman has given birth to a daughter as a result of fertility treatment, Adriana Iliescu [the mother] seems to be no Earth Mother figure prevented by tragic circumstances from having the family she deserved. She is single; a retired university professor who claims to have been too busy pursuing her career to get around to having babies earlier in life.

Ms Iliescu's newfound status as World's Oldest Mum has attracted consternation across the UK [United Kingdom] press, to whom the photographic contrast of little Eliza Maria [the baby] and the wrinkled face of her ageing mother has proved irresistible. It's not natural, apparently, to have a baby at this age; and moreover it's a really, really selfish thing to do. Maybe so—but what business is it of ours how a Romanian retiree chooses to plan her family?

In today's disoriented moral universe, stories such as that of Ms Iliescu invariably provide an opportunity for yet more commentary on what kind of people should be able to have children, and for what reasons. The UK's 'oldest mum' stories—such as 60-year-old Liz Buttle, who gave birth to a son in 1997, and the 59-year-old grandmother from Surrey who has recently had two small children—found their fertility choices under a similar spotlight.

It is taken for granted that these women's desire to take advantage of new technology to buck the biological clock says something disturbing about the way we view parenting and children today. In fact, the disturbing trend lies less in the private choices made by elderly mums than in the public discussion about them.

Fertility Treatments Are All Unnatural

Of course it is not natural for a menopausal woman to have children using somebody else's eggs. But no fertility treatment is natural—that's the whole point of it. Our society thankfully accepts that, for young women who are biologically incapable of conceiving or carrying children, or for young men who have suffered from cancer, say, or some other cause of infertility, IVF provides a wonderful opportunity to bypass the unfairness meted out by nature.

We've come a long way from the ethical outpourings that greeted the birth of the UK's first 'test tube baby', Louise Brown, in the 1970s. Fertility treatment is now commonplace and for the most part uncontroversial, and too many people know too many couples who have benefited from IVF to fail to recognise the joy it can bring. By the same token, people are also very aware of the problems of IVF. Far from being some kind of miracle, as it is often portrayed, which enables any woman to have as many babies as she wants whenever she wants, IVF remains an unpleasant, unreliable procedure that can be ruinously expensive and cause a great deal of heartache.

But even to be given a shot at IVF today, you have to be deemed the right sort of person. If you are too old, too poor, too single, too gay or too greedy (in the sense that you demand maximising your chances of success by having 'too many' embryos implanted at once), you are considered fair game for all manner of moral opprobrium. It is as though the biological barriers an individual faces to having children makes it only natural that their emotions, motivations and social status should be scrutinised and, often, condemned.

Research Backs Older Mothers

"Women over 50 who give birth can be just as good as younger women when it comes to motherhood, say researchers from the University of California, at the [2006] annual meeting of the American Society for Reproductive Medicines. There is no evidence that women in their fifties experience higher levels of stress or experience greater health risks, compared to younger women who give birth. The researchers examined data on 150 mothers who had received fertility treatment between 1992–2004. . . . The women were surveyed to determine their physical and mental functioning and parental stress. Their findings revealed that the women in their 50s were not less capable as parents—neither did they experience higher levels of stress than the other women. The researchers suggest that public prejudice is the problem, not poor capacity on the part of older mothers."

Christian Nordqvist, Medical News Today, *October 23, 2006.*

Intrusive Oversight

In the UK, prospective parents seeking fertility treatment have to pass a complex series of suitability tests laid down by the Human Fertilisation and Embryology Authority (HFEA), laying their lives open to official scrutiny in a way that would be unthinkable for parents who conceive naturally. The HFEA is apparently now looking at relaxing some of these rules, making it easier for single parents and gay couples to access treatment—but this is reportedly likely to be accompanied by stiffer regulations to check for criminal records and to restrict the number of babies a woman can have at any one time.

Add to this the news headlines that generally greet the birth of an IVF baby to somebody who falls short of the parenting ideal, and one wonders what makes these new parents so different that they can invite such interference and contempt.

Parenting Is Selfish

The answer, of course, is nothing. There is nothing profoundly different between parents of IVF children and those who conceive naturally. The only difference is that couples who use IVF are an easier target for those wishing to moralise about the problem of parents in general, with their apparently dodgy desires and 'wrong' life choices.

Given modern society's appreciation of contraception and overall sympathy towards fertility treatment, the cry that 'it's not natural' for a grandmother-figure to start dropping sprogs [children] is not particularly convincing. The problem that preoccupies most commentators, therefore, is that Ms Iliescu's decision to do so is selfish. 'When this Romanian girl is 21, her mother will be 87', proclaims the front page of the *Guardian* [Manchester].

'[A] woman who is 67 when she conceives is more likely to be a burden than a guardian to her child: in her 80s, her health and energy level will fall short of meeting the demands of a teenager', writes Cristina Odone in *The Times* (London). Ms Iliescu, like all the other high-profile elderly mums we read about, is branded guilty of the heinous crime of putting her own desire for a child ahead of what is presumed to be in the child's best interests.

This argument has a number of logical flaws. Is it, then, in Eliza Maria's best interests not to be born? Has that minority of children born to biological parents but raised by their grandparents over the generations been somehow damaged by grandad's inability to play football at weekends and grandma's stroke? If it is selfish to have a child because you are older than the other parents, surely it is selfish to have a child when your house is smaller than it could be and your salary is less than you would like it to be? However you do it, having children is essentially a selfish thing to do—nobody, surely, decides to get pregnant for the benefit of that particular egg, and many people routinely take a great deal of effort to avoid getting pregnant accidentally.

Teen Mums Also Slammed

And for all the talk about the problem with older mums, it's worth reminding ourselves that Britain today shows even less tolerance towards teenagers who become mothers—despite the fact that their 'health and energy levels' are at their peak, in marked contrast to the sleep-deprived thirtysomething mother 'juggling' work and life, that darling of media and policymaking circles. While many of us may not imagine wanting to choose motherhood while drawing our pension (or indeed while still receiving pocket money), none of the apparently principled arguments against it makes any sense.

It is one thing to have a debate about whether women having children in their 60s is really something to celebrate: and this would be an interesting debate to have. It is another thing entirely to use spurious arguments about extreme cases such as these to push for the need for yet more regulation of parents' fertility decisions, as though the treatment of one elderly Romanian woman is the top of a slippery slope towards irresponsible behaviour by anybody seeking fertility treatment.

Above all, we should recognise that the emphasis placed upon the welfare of a putative child in such discussions, whether the child is conceived naturally or as a consequence of IVF, is one of society's big lies. It is a cover for officials and commentators to air their prejudices about what kind of people should become parents, and how they should raise their children. Whether a woman is 60 or 16, she, and not some committee, is best placed to make the choice about the kind of family she wants to have.

> "Despite the difficulties with conceiving and having a normal, healthy child [after age forty], the increased complication to the mother is also cause for alarm."

Older Women Should Be Discouraged from Using Reproductive Technologies to Become Mothers

Jamie Borland

In the following viewpoint Jamie Borland argues for regulations to require postmenopausal women to undergo rigorous medical testing and psychological counseling before becoming pregnant through in vitro fertilization (IVF). Borland points out that health complications are more likely for older women using reproductive technologies. Additionally, she points out, there is a likelihood that an older woman will not survive long enough to assure that her child is fully grown and capable of being self-supporting. Considering that the state will have to care for orphans of postmenopausal mothers, Borland argues that the government should prevent older women from using IVF unless they

Jamie Borland, "What Every Oklahoma Elder Lawyer Should Know about Postmenopausal Pregnancy," *Elder Law: A Compendium of Materials*, December 1, 2003. Reproduced by permission.

can prove that they understand its implications and can meet all the requirements of independent motherhood at an advanced age. At the time of writing, Jamie Borland was a student at the University of Oklahoma College of Law. She is now an attorney in Oklahoma.

As you read, consider the following questions:

1. Does the right to conceive mean that there is a right to fertility treatments, in Borland's view?
2. What factor does the author think is contributing to the rise in infertile women?
3. What requirements would Borland impose on fertility clinics?

With the increase in life expectancy and the increase in women pursuing higher education and long-term careers, the traditional family model has been thrown out. Fertility treatments that were not even heard of twenty years ago are now becoming very successful at allowing those who had no chance of conceiving children to conceive and bear healthy children. Coupled with the desire of women in their 40's and 50's to have children, the result has been a marked increase in children born to postmenopausal women. . . .

No Right to Fertility

The Supreme Court has held that "marriage and procreation are fundamental to the very existence and survival of the race", *Skinner v. Oklahoma*, 316 U.S. 535, at 541 (1942). Through other cases, such as *Roe v. Wade, Planned Parenthood of Southeastern Pennsylvania v. Casey,* and *Griswold v. Connecticut,* the privacy rights of a family to make decisions concerning marriage, procreation, and the like have been made clear. There should not be unjustified government intrusion.

While the right to conceive and bear children remains clear in the courtroom, what is not clear is that very right when a woman cannot conceive by herself. There is no fundamental right to fertility treatments. Medicaid and other state funds will not approve the use of state money for fertility treatments, leaving those who cannot afford the expensive procedures little options of conceiving. Therefore, at the present time, only those who can actually afford the procedures are able to utilize them, and they can be quite expensive. According to a mid-1990's study, the average costs for in-vitro fertilization are between $66,000 and $114,000. Moreover, the cost of actually delivering a baby ranges from $160,000 to $180,000 when IVF has been used to overcome postmenopausal age. This allows for only affluent couples or women to conceive, or those willing to deplete their life savings. . . .

After menopause, a woman stops producing eggs. It is only through methods such as in-vitro fertilization (IVF) that conception is possible. The question becomes whether a woman, after menopause, should be allowed access to these fertility treatments. Since there is little regulation in the field of fertility treatments, possibly due to the government's fear of infringing on rights the court has deemed private, clinics are left to regulate themselves. Some clinics require very low standards (other than the requisite ability to pay), others are very strict, requiring good health and imposing age limitations. . . .

Many Women Wait

Once a woman has surpassed the age of 40, her chances of becoming pregnant are cut in half. By age 42, the chance of miscarriage increases to 50 percent and the chance for having a child with chromosomal abnormalities such as Down syndrome increases dramatically. Despite the difficulties with conceiving and having a normal, healthy child, the increased complication to the mother is also cause for alarm. Women over forty are three times more likely to develop gestational diabetes, and there is a 40 percent increase in the number of cesarean sections.

On the other hand, because of advances in fertility-enhancing therapies, the number of births to mothers age 50 and over is growing. Why are women waiting so long before thinking about having a family? More and more women are pursuing careers first. While some women start their families early on before careers, some women are waiting until retirement to have children. Fertility clinics are now full of women who are at postmenopausal age, and every year there are more. A study in 1995 found that in seven years—from 1988 to 1995—the number of American women in their childbearing years who suffered from infertility went from 4.9 [million] to 6.1 million, a 25 percent jump, in part because many women are waiting longer to have their children. . . .

Need for Regulation

There should be regulation in the field of reproductive technology. Just what that regulation should be poses another question. There are arguments for both sides. Those for regulation argue that a woman's biological age limit (through menopause) should not be extended just because the technology is available. Others argue that the health risks to mother and child are too great to allow unregulated treatment. European countries have already banned the use of IVF's for women past menopause.

Other concerns are whether the mother's mental capacity will continue through child rearing. Studies indicate that women are significantly more likely than men to be hospitalized for a mental disorder. Women and men studied between the ages of 65–74 showed that women were 30% more likely to be hospitalized for a mental disorder. This raises the chances of older women to orphan or psychologically affect a child.

Aside from the health complications which exist for the mother, there is also the increase in the chance of a child having a chromosomal disorder. This increased risk is based on the age of the eggs and the health of the mother. Many chil-

"I took my parents for granted until I had kids of my own. I don't know what I'd do if they weren't here to raise them."

dren born with these disorders require an immense amount of care and money. A parent will have to be able to deal with the emotional and financial hardships of raising a child with a disability at a time when they should be focusing on saving money for their retirement. If the money is not there, who is going to pay? If the older couple has spent their money on fertility treatments, how much can be left to pay for the child's expenses, college, retirement, nursing facilities. Also, many

IVF's result in multiple births, so not only are the parents bearing the cost of one child, [but] in many cases, there are two or more children. If the child is orphaned at a young age, the chance of the child becoming a ward of the state increases, especially if the child is afflicted with a disorder. Then the state is left to pay the expenses. Also, the state may be left paying the expenses for a child that is the ward of the state through Medicaid, as well as nursing facilities for the parent if they are no longer able to care for themselves.

Some women age 63 are giving birth for the first time. Even if the mother reaches the ripe old age of 83, the child will only be twenty. It is very unlikely that the mother will be able to meet her grandchildren. In essence, the mother has bypassed having children and went straight to being a grandmother. While it is true that many grandparents are being forced to raise children of their children due to many factors such as death of the child, drug abuse, or incarceration, it has also been shown that it can be an extreme hardship on grandparents to raise children. Plus, this is an option that children whose parents are elderly will not have. As in the case above, if the child at age 30 has a child, the mother will be 93. There is no way that the 93-year-old grandmother will be able to take care of the grandchild should the mother pass away. This again leaves the State to take up the bill. . . .

Counseling Should Be Mandatory

It is my proposition that fertility clinics should be required to screen their patients through a series of tests and counseling. Before a postmenopausal woman should be able to conceive, she should first be physically fit with no history of serious life threatening disease. . . . This includes blood tests, stress treadmill and chest X-ray. Though it is a step, there should be a psychological component as well. A woman should be required to participate in counseling regarding the possible implications of her decision. Has she considered the increased risk to her health as well as her child's? Is she aware of the chance that she will not conceive despite the treatments? Is she capable of handling the financial burden of ARTs [assisted reproductive technologies]? One should also consider why a woman past menopause has chosen to have a child; is it the fear that she is missing something? Has she married later in life? Has she been focusing on a career instead of a family? We live in a society today where we are told that we can have it all, we can do it all, and we should do it all. For those women who have "chosen" to have an education and a career, motherhood was postponed in lieu of the career. They can now "choose" to have a child, and in essence, have it all.

A woman should also have an idea of who will take care of the child should something happen to her. Who will bear the burden of taking care of both the mother and the child should the mother fall ill? And, who will be able to make decisions concerning the estate should the mother pass on while the child is still a minor? It may also be beneficial for the mother to show that she is financially capable of raising a child born through the use of IVF as well as financially capable of taking care of herself into old age. Even though these issues do not have to be addressed when a mother chooses to conceive naturally, it should be the government's responsibility to insure that treatments are not given to women who cannot handle the responsibility or are physically incapable of doing so.

"The government, working in coopera-tion with embryo adoption organiza-tions, should form and implement a legislative framework to minimize the legal ramifications associated with em-bryo adoption."

The Government Should Support Embryo Adoptions

Daniel I. Wallance

In the following viewpoint Daniel I. Wallance cites the advan-tages of embryo adoption for infertile couples. Using a frozen embryo to start a pregnancy is less invasive and expensive than in vitro fertilization (IVF), he claims. It also provides couples with more control over the gestation and birth of their adoptive child than is possible in ordinary adoption. Embryo adoption, he argues, should be supported by the government to help reduce the vast numbers of frozen embryos left over from IVF. While still an undergraduate student at the Worcester Polytechnic Insti-tute, Daniel I. Wallance created the report from which this ex-cerpt is drawn at the suggestion of one of the founders of the Center for Adoption Policy Studies. He has since earned his bachelor's degree and become chief information officer for the center.

Daniel I. Wallance, "Defrosting Embryo Adoption," *Center for Adoption Policy*, De-cember 17, 2003. Reproduced by permission.

As you read, consider the following questions:

1. What, according to Wallance, is a leading cause of large numbers of unused frozen embryos?
2. How does the author classify an embryo donated to an infertile couple?
3. What step should doctors take, in Wallance's view, to reduce the supply of frozen embryos?

The strong emotion felt by the biological parents in deciding whether to put their embryos up for adoption, destroy them, or donate them for research is only appropriately viewed when contrasted with the satisfaction gained by the adoptive parents. . . .

Couples usually choose embryo adoption at a point when other options, including in-vitro fertilization, fail and when traditional adoption is undesirable. "Embryo adoption is an option for couples who want to share a pregnancy experience and have neither eggs nor sperm to contribute to that process," say Susan Cooper and Ellen Glazer (1998) in their book, *Choosing Assisted Reproduction*. They want to experience pregnancy. The mother wants to know what it is like to give birth, to feel the baby kicking inside her. Embryo adoption provides a form of therapy to couples who continually struggle with their infertility while watching others become pregnant and give birth to beautiful babies. . . .

Wealth of Medical Data

In embryo adoption, even if the adopting couple receives comforting information of a clean medical history, the nature of the adoption provides for an additional level of forewarning. In most cases, the biological parents had leftover embryos from in-vitro fertilization because they stopped treatment once the mother gave birth. Since the frozen embryos received by the adopting couple are genetic siblings of the biological parents' child, any genetic disorders or medical problems dis-

President Bush Backs Embryo Adoption

"With the right policies and the right techniques, we can pursue scientific progress while still fulfilling our moral duties. I want to thank Nightlight Christian Adoptions for their good work. Nightlight's embryo adoption program has now matched over 200 biological parents with about 140 adoptive families, resulting in the birth of 81 children so far, with more on the way. . . . The children here today remind us that there is no such thing as a spare embryo. Every embryo is unique and genetically complete, like every other human being. And each of us started out our life this way. These lives are not raw material to be exploited, but gifts. And I commend each of the families here today for accepting the gift of these children and offering them the gift of your love."

George W. Bush, "President Discusses Embryo Adoption and Ethical Stem Cell Research," May 24, 2005. www.whitehouse.gov.

covered from the child can be relayed to the adopting couple to let them know what could progress. . . .

In traditional adoption, couples seek the after product. The couple can examine the child they are interested in adopting and have the option of deciding whether to adopt. With embryo adoption there is no turning back. At the same time, in traditional adoption medical aliments could be hidden.

Adoptive parents should also consider the benefits of being able to control the birth cycle. In traditional adoption there is no guarantee the biological mother did not consume drugs and or alcohol during the pregnancy. The female adoptive parent, pregnant from another couple's previously frozen embryo, takes on the responsibility of ensuring a pregnancy environment in which the fetus receives enough nutrients and no harmful substances. . . .

Need Will Persist

As long as infertility remains an unpleasant fact of life, couples will continue to seek in-vitro fertilization. Traditional adoption is an easier and possibly less complicated solution, but couples desire biological children of their own and one method is through in-vitro fertilization. For in-vitro fertilization to be a cost-effective solution, doctors will continue to produce excessive amounts of embryos for a couple and cryogenically [by freezing] store the unused. Consequently, the quantity of frozen embryos in storage will only grow higher. The larger number of frozen embryos translates to a greater availability for infertile couples seeking to adopt embryos. Even with the astonishing number of frozen embryos stored today, the hesitancy of couples to give away their embryos results in a shortage of those available for adoption. If the number in storage increases, then the percentage available to adoptive couples will also increase. . . .

Government Backing Could Help

The unquestionable growth of this controversial industry will uproot legal and ethical consequences. The government, working in cooperation with embryo adoption organizations, should form and implement a legislative framework to minimize the legal ramifications associated with embryo adoption, including the rights of the biological and adoptive parents. One major point is whether infertility clinics can release embryos for adoption when the biological parents are unreachable. Already the government is showing interest in embryo adoption. President [George W.] Bush in 2002 developed plans to distribute approximately one million dollars to organizations such as Snowflakes in an effort to promote embryo adoption. Although monetary support is beneficial, long-term sustainability will hold if embryo adoption organizations receive the support of a legislative framework based upon the current practices of traditional adoption, including home studies. . . .

Adoption as a Solution

Infertility clinics will continue to produce excess frozen embryos as long as in-vitro fertilization remains a popular treatment for infertile couples. Infertile couples possessing excess embryos must make an immediate and definitive decision regarding their embryos' fate at the point when further children are undesirable and an initial IVF treatment was successful. I believe it is unfair and unhealthy for the biological parents to postpone their decision. The high number of frozen embryos currently in storage is partly a result of indecision. Embryo adoption therefore provides an excellent solution.

Organizations such as Snowflakes, who base embryo adoption on the model of traditional adoption, use an appropriate approach. I feel this procedure is desirable for satisfying the emotional needs of the biological parents and therefore encourages their participation. . . .

I believe the frozen embryos should be classified as providing an infertile adoptive couple the potential for a child based on the low probability for success in embryo adoption. I do not even support the definition that a frozen embryo provides a couple with a potential child. Embryo adoption should not provide any ammunition to support pro-life groups nor should it provide any ammunition to support pro-choice. Society should view embryo adoption simply as an appropriate mechanism by which to distribute existing frozen embryos to infertile couples.

Although I support embryo adoption, I do not feel embryo donation is appropriate so long as frozen embryos remain in storage. In embryo donation physicians use separately donated gametes to form new embryos. The purpose of embryo adoption is to appropriately use and distribute existing frozen embryos. Embryo donation works against embryo adoption since physicians create new embryos instead of using those already in existence. As long as frozen embryos remain in storage, physicians should avoid embryo donation and couples with frozen embryos, unsure of their decision, should be encouraged to decide.

Restraint on Embryo Production

Biological parents must also work to reduce the amount of newly frozen embryos by minimizing the number produced during their in-vitro fertilization trials. I am not saying that physicians should produce and implant only one embryo at a time, but the quantity needs to decrease. At the same time, physicians should not place the health of the biological mother at an elevated risk. Decreasing the quantity of embryos produced must be weighted against the success rates of a live birth and therefore minimizing the need for extracting subsequent eggs and further stimulatory drugs. Although this might be the present goal of in-vitro fertilization clinics, economic benefits and the couple's possible interest in raising more children at a later date should not play a part. With approximately 400,000 frozen embryos currently in storage, practices need to change.

I believe embryo adoption is a worthwhile solution requiring the full support of embryo adoption clinics, infertile couples with frozen embryos, infertile couples seeking frozen embryos, the government, fertility clinics, reproductive specialists, adoption policy groups, and traditional adoption agencies to provide guidance.

> "[Government money] would be far better spent matching fertile couples willing to make embryos with infertile couples, rather than trying to get them to use unhealthy frozen ones."

Embryo Adoptions Are a Waste of Government Money

Arthur Caplan

In the following selection, bioethicist Arthur Caplan argues that embryo adoptions are not a genuine boon but rather a cover for an ideology about the status of embryos. The Nightlight Christian Adoption agency, which runs a government-funded embryo adoption program called Snowflakes, acts out of the belief that embryos are babies, Caplan says. Using the language of adoption may mislead prospective parents, he claims, and questions why anyone would want to adopt an embryo that was rejected as inferior during the process of in vitro fertilization. Arthur Caplan is director of the Center for Bioethics at the University of Pennsylvania in Philadelphia.

As you read, consider the following questions:

1. What about the qualifications of the Nightlight Christian Adoption agency makes Caplan skeptical?

Arthur Caplan, "The Problem with 'Embryo Adoption'," MSNBC, June 24, 2003. www.msnbc.msn.com. Reproduced by permission.

2. What are the chances that an embryo frozen less than five years will become a baby, in the author's view?

3. How does Caplan think the government investment in embryo adoption could be better used?

One of the strangest outcomes of the ongoing debate over embryonic stem-cell research is the government's use of taxpayer money to support a little-known private organization called Snowflakes. Devoted to encouraging couples to "adopt" human embryos, Snowflakes has received over $1 million from the [George W.] Bush administration and Congress.

While helping people have babies is ethically commendable, there is something very strange about extending the use of the term "adoption" to embryos. Children get adopted, but . . . embryos?

And it is even stranger that the federal government is buying into this way of thinking.

So where do all these embryos that supposedly need adopting come from in the first place?

Embryo Production

When couples seek treatment for infertility, they often wind up using in-vitro fertilization, or IVF. This is a procedure in which embryos are created outside the body in a laboratory dish and are then implanted back into the woman's body where, ideally, they grow to full term.

It works like this: The woman takes fertility drugs that cause her to produce far more eggs than the one she normally would release during her monthly cycle. These eggs are then surgically removed from her ovaries and fertilized in a dish with either her husband's or a donor's sperm.

Often many embryos are created through this process. But since multiple-pregnancies—quadruplets, quintuplets, septuplets and the like—produce premature and often unhealthy

A Tiny Fraction of Embryos Are Adoptable

"Fertility clinics across the country, according to the most recent data available, held about 400,000 frozen embryos as of May 2003. Patients had reserved 88 percent of them for their own future use, and they had earmarked about 3 percent for medical research. Two percent—or about 9,000 embryos—were available for donation to other couples, according to Sean Tipton, director of public affairs at the American Society for Reproductive Medicine, which collected the data. Nobody knows for sure how many embryos have actually been donated, or how many children have been born as a result, but the numbers appear to be relatively small. . . . Proponents of embryonic stem cell research, which requires the destruction of the embryos but which many scientists think has enormous potential to develop ways to repair organs and fight disease, say there are so few adoptions that thousands of embryos will be discarded if they are not used for research."

Alan Cooperman,
Washington Post, *May 31, 2005.*

babies, doctors will only put two or three embryos back into the woman's body to try and help her become pregnant.

The clinic chooses to implant the embryos that look the healthiest and asks the couple if they want to freeze the rest. The couple also has the option of having the remaining embryos destroyed, donated to other couples, or donated for embryonic stem-cell research.

The Snowflakes Program

This is where Snowflakes saw a need—and a chance to score some moral points in the debate over stem-cell research.

Snowflakes is run by the Nightlight Christian Adoption agency in Fullerton, Calif. The group has no medical background. They simply believe that every embryo is a baby from the minute it exists in a laboratory dish.

The Snowflakes program deliberately uses the language of adoption to make that point clear. They created a service that matches couples who have leftover embryos with other infertile couples trying to have babies. To quote from their [literature]: "By some estimates, there are over 100,000 frozen embryos in cryo-banks throughout the United States. Pre-born children waiting—waiting."

Actually Snowflakes' estimate of 100,000 embryos is probably very low. Most experts think there are as many as 400,000 embryos frozen in storage in the United States. As of [2002], the Snowflakes program had received about 750 of them and had matched 70 donor couples with 48 other couples seeking to have children. Sixteen babies had been born.

Creating False Impressions

So what's the big deal about a religious group that believes all embryos are children and is trying to find them "adoptive" parents among infertile couples using IVF? Well, actually there is a lot that is wrong.

It's great that 16 babies were born through the Snowflakes program. That makes it seem as if 16 couples had children who might otherwise have not. But that is not really the case. Nearly all infertility clinics offer couples the option of donating their leftover embryos to other couples. All that Snowflakes has done is brought the rhetoric of adoption into the process.

You might also get the impression that Snowflakes is creating an opportunity for infertile couples to access the 100,000 to 400,000 frozen embryos out there. But that is not really the case either. If you are infertile and are trying to have a baby, your best bet is not to use a frozen embryo made by a couple who had themselves been going through infertility treatment and whose embryos were not used because they did not look healthy enough.

Slim Chance of Survival

Despite Snowflakes' rhetoric, most frozen embryos are not healthy enough to ever become babies. The chance they will grow to full term is about one in 10 for those frozen less than five years, and even less for those that have been frozen longer. This is why so few couples have taken Snowflakes up on its idea of "adopting" frozen embryos.

Moreover, using terms like "adoption" encourages people to believe that frozen embryos are the equivalent of children. But they are not the same. In fact, infertile couples who want children can frequently make embryos but they cannot make embryos that become fetuses or babies.

The older a woman gets, the less likely her embryos are to become babies. For women over 45, the chance of her embryo becoming a baby is almost zero. The inability to make embryos that become babies is why couples turn to donor eggs or donor sperm. Almost no one who is going to spend $10,000 per try to use IVF is going to want to try it with another infertile couple's frozen embryo whose chances of properly developing grow less with every year it is frozen.

Misspent Money

The Bush administration and Congress know all these facts, but have nevertheless poured more than $1 million of taxpayer money into the Snowflakes program and others aimed at facilitating "embryo adoption."

This is a nice way to score points with those who advocate the view that embryos are actual babies and should not be used for research purposes. But it is not the best way to help couples who want to have actual babies.

One million dollars would be far better spent matching fertile couples willing to make embryos with infertile couples, rather than trying to get them to use unhealthy frozen ones.

One million dollars could also help defray the staggering costs of IVF, which only middle- and upper-class couples can currently afford.

But when the money is spent on programs like Snow-flakes, the only explanation is ideology not medicine.

Periodical Bibliography

The following articles have been selected to supplement the diverse views presented in this chapter.

Shaoni Bhattacharya   "Electronic Tags for Eggs, Sperm and Embryos," *New Scientist*, March 30, 2005. www.newscientist.com/article.ns?id=dn7209.

B.J. Erb   "Deconstructing the Human Egg: The FDA's Regulation of Scientifically Created Babies," *Roger Williams University Law Review*, Fall 1999.

Ethics Committee of the American Society for Reproductive Medicine   "Preconception Gender Selection for Nonmedical Reasons," *Fertility and Sterility*, May 2001. www.asrm.org/Media/Ethics/preconception gender.pdf.

Karla Gale   "Assisted Reproduction 'Reasonable' Until Age 44," *Reuters Health*, August 22, 2005. http://today.reuters.co.uk/news/newsArticle.aspx?type=healthNews&storyID=2005-08-22T17 3303Z_01_SCH263109_RTRIDST_0_HEALTH-ASSISTED-REPRODUCTION-DC.XML.

Paul R. Gindoff   "Fertility Management in the Older Woman," RESOLVE. www.resolve.org/site/PageServer?pagename=pubs_fmow.

Kirsty Horsey   "UK Government Proposes New Laws on Assisted Reproduction," BioNews.com, December 17, 2006. www.bionews.org.uk/new.lasso?storyid=3291.

Lori P. Knowles   "Reprogenetics: A Chance for Meaningful Regulation," *Hastings Center Report*, May–June 2002.

OPPOSING
VIEWPOINTS®
SERIES

CHAPTER 4

Should New Reproductive Technologies Be Pursued?

Chapter Preface

Reproductive technologies are rapidly evolving. Even those who are comfortable with today's practices are awestruck by the prospects of future developments. The two possibilities that engender the greatest concern are "designer baby" technologies and human reproductive cloning.

The term "designer baby" refers to the possibility that through genetic engineering certain desirable genes, such as those for height, eye color, or intelligence, might be inserted into the genome of an embryo. Proponents of this kind of technology say that genetic engineering could eliminate a host of genetic defects and diseases. Who would want their baby to be born with a fatal condition such as cystic fibrosis if it could be prevented and the gene for it eliminated forever? Proponents say that holding back the development of such technology will only increase needless suffering in the world.

Opponents of human genetic engineering argue that it will lead to competition among parents to buy the best "designer genes" for their offspring. The wealthy will gain an unfair genetic advantage over the rest of us, they argue. Political scientist Francis Fukuyama in his book *Our Posthuman Future* has gone so far as to argue that it will mean the end of human nature.

An even fiercer controversy rages over the possibility of human reproductive cloning. The idea that someone could donate an ordinary cell, have its genetic contents inserted into a hollowed-out egg cell, and then proceed to implant the resulting embryo in a womb frightens and outrages many people. On the other hand, the prospect that a child killed in an accident could be reborn, at least in a genetically identical baby, is a wonderful vision in the eyes of some.

It must be emphasized that human reproductive cloning is an unproven and uncertain technology. Animal experiments with cloning have had uneven results. Many miscarriages have occurred, and live offspring have frequently shown signs of premature aging and genetic disorders. Given this record, even to experiment with human reproductive cloning would be highly unethical, many critics argue.

If cloning were safe and reliable, it would still face considerable opposition. Many religious traditions are against it. Many Christian denominations have come out in opposition. Islamic clerics differ among themselves on the question. Saudi Arabia's Sheikh Mohammad ibn Saleh al-Othimin, a member of the country's highest religious council, has called for amputation or death for scientists engaged in cloning. "It amounts to manipulation of humankind," he has been quoted as saying, "It's the worst kind of corruption on earth." On the other hand, Lebanon's Shi'ite leader Sheikh Mohammad Hussein Fadlallah, concludes that "it is false to say that cloning is an attempt to intervene in the divine creation," because in his view God allowed such discoveries to be made in order to further divine purposes.

Opinion polls show greater public opposition to human reproductive cloning than to any other reproductive technology. A 2002 poll of Americans found that 77 percent opposed human reproductive cloning, while only 17 percent favored it. Even most scientists oppose reproductive cloning, at least for now. A 2002 National Academy of Sciences panel concluded that a ban on reproductive cloning should remain in place for at least five years.

Many scientists, however, do support therapeutic, or research, cloning, a process in which an embryo is created but never implanted. Instead, it is used to produce stem cells, which have the potential to become any human organ. Stem cell research, biomedical researchers argue, promises to produce a great new wave of cures. Nevertheless, even this limited form of cloning faces strong opposition, especially from religious quarters. It is moving forward in some countries but has lagged in the United States due mainly to a ban on federal funding for such research.

Science advances on many fronts, however, and cloning proponents claim that it is only a matter of time before someone successfully clones a human being. Once the barrier is crossed, they say, others will inevitably follow.

"Research cloning gives man too much power for evil."

Research Cloning Is a Threat

Charles Krauthammer

In the viewpoint that follows, Charles Krauthammer argues that allowing research cloning to go forward would be wrong because it would inevitably lead to reproductive cloning. Furthermore, he argues, even if an embryo is not regarded as sacred, it deserves respect. Otherwise, he fears people will go down a slippery ethical slope to harming fetuses or infants, use the power of cloning for evil purposes, or simply lose respect for human life. Charles Krauthammer is a Pulitzer Prize–winning neoconservative news commentator, a psychiatrist, and a former member of the President's Council on Bioethics.

As you read, consider the following questions:

1. Why does Krauthammer reject the term "therapeutic cloning?"
2. In the author's opinion, what moral absurdity could research cloning lead to if reproductive cloning remains illegal?

Charles Krauthammer, "A Secular Argument Against Research Cloning: Crossing Lines," *The New Republic*, April 22, 2002. Copyright © 2002 by The New Republic, Inc. Reproduced by permission of *The New Republic*.

3. What horrifying vision of the future does Krauthammer foresee if mass production of clones is permitted?

You were once a single cell. Every one of the 100 trillion cells in your body today is a direct descendent of that zygote, the primordial cell formed by the union of mother's egg and father's sperm. Each one is genetically identical (allowing for copying errors and environmental damage along the way) to that cell. Therefore, if we scraped a cell from, say, the inner lining of your cheek, its DNA would be the same DNA that, years ago in the original zygote, contained the entire plan for creating you and every part of you.

Here is the mystery: Why can the zygote, as it multiplies, produce every different kind of cell in the body—kidney, liver, brain, skin—while the skin cell is destined, however many times it multiplies, to remain skin forever? As the embryo matures, cells become specialized and lose their flexibility and plasticity. Once an adult cell has specialized-differentiated, in scientific lingo—it is stuck forever in that specialty. Skin is skin; kidney is kidney.

Understanding that mystery holds the keys to the kingdom. The Holy Grail of modern biology is regenerative medicine. If we can figure out how to make a specialized adult cell dedifferentiate—unspecialize, i.e., revert way back to the embryonic stage, perhaps even to the original zygotic stage—and then grow it like an embryo under controlled circumstances, we could reproduce for you every kind of tissue or organ you might need. We could create a storehouse of repair parts for your body. And, if we let that dedifferentiated cell develop completely in a woman's uterus, we will have created a copy of you, your clone.

That is the promise and the menace of cloning. It has already been done in sheep, mice, goats, pigs, cows, and now cats and rabbits (though cloning rabbits seems an exercise in biological redundancy). There is no reason in principle why it cannot be done in humans. The question is: Should it be done? . . .

The Promise

This is how research cloning works. You take a donor egg from a woman, remove its nucleus, and inject the nucleus of, say, a skin cell from another person. It has been shown in animals that by the right manipulation you can trick the egg and the injected nucleus into dedifferentiating—that means giving up all the specialization of the skin cell and returning to its original state as a primordial cell that could become anything in the body.

In other words, this cell becomes totipotent. It becomes the equivalent of the fertilized egg in normal procreation, except that instead of having chromosomes from two people, it has chromosomes from one. This cell then behaves precisely like an embryo. It divides. It develops. At four to seven days, it forms a "blastocyst" consisting of about 100 to 200 cells.

The main objective of cloning researchers would be to disassemble this blastocyst: pull the stem cells out, grow them in the laboratory, and then try to tease them into becoming specific kinds of cells, say, kidney or heart or brain and so on.

There would be two purposes for doing this: study or cure. You could take a cell from a person with a baffling disease, like Lou Gehrig's, clone it into a blastocyst, pull the stem cells out, and then study them in order to try to understand the biology of the illness. Or you could begin with a cell from a person with Parkinson's or a spinal cord injury, clone it, and tease out the stem cells to develop tissue that you would reinject into the original donor to, in theory, cure the Parkinson's or spinal cord injury. The advantage of using a cloned cell rather than an ordinary stem cell is that, presumably, there would be no tissue rejection. It's your own DNA. The body would recognize it. You'd have a perfect match.

(Research cloning is sometimes called therapeutic cloning, but that is a misleading term. First, because therapy by reinjection is only one of the many uses to which this cloning can be put. Moreover, it is not therapeutic for the clone—indeed, the clone is invariably destroyed in the process—though it may be therapeutic for others. If you donate a kidney to your brother, it would be odd to call your operation a therapeutic nephrectomy. It is not. It's a sacrificial nephrectomy.)

Rejection Problem

The conquest of rejection is one of the principal rationales for research cloning. But there is reason to doubt this claim on scientific grounds. There is some empirical evidence in mice that cloned tissue may be rejected anyway (possibly because a clone contains a small amount of foreign—mitochondrial—DNA derived from the egg into which it was originally injected). Moreover, enormous advances are being made elsewhere in combating tissue rejection. The science of immune rejection is much more mature than the science of cloning. By the time we figure out how to do safe and reliable research cloning, the rejection problem may well be solved. And finally, there are less problematic alternatives—such as adult stem cells—that offer a promising alternative to cloning because they present no problem of tissue rejection and raise none of cloning's moral conundrums.

These scientific considerations raise serious questions about the efficacy of, and thus the need for, research cloning. But there is a stronger case to be made. Even if the scientific objections are swept aside, even if research cloning is as doable and promising as its advocates contend, there are other reasons to pause.

The most obvious is this: Research cloning is an open door to reproductive cloning. Banning the production of cloned babies while permitting the production of cloned embryos makes no sense. If you have factories all around the country producing embryos for research and commerce, it is inevitable that someone will implant one in a woman (or perhaps in some artificial medium in the farther future) and produce a human clone. What then? A law banning reproductive cloning but permitting research cloning would then make it a crime not to destroy that fetus—an obvious moral absurdity.

This is an irrefutable point and the reason that many in Congress will vote for the total ban on cloning. Philosophically, however, it is a showstopper. It lets us off too early and too easy. It keeps us from facing the deeper question: Is there anything about research cloning that in and of itself makes it morally problematic?

Intrinsic Worth

For some people, life begins at conception. And not just life—if life is understood to mean a biologically functioning organism, even a single cell is obviously alive—but personhood. If the first zygotic cell is owed all the legal and moral respect due a person, then there is nothing to talk about. Ensoulment starts with Day One and Cell One, and the idea of taking that cell or its successor cells apart to serve someone else's needs is abhorrent.

This is an argument of great moral force but little intellectual interest. Not because it may not be right. But because it is unprovable. It rests on metaphysics. Either you believe it or you don't. The discussion ends there.

I happen not to share this view. I do not believe personhood begins at conception. I do not believe a single cell has the moral or legal standing of a child. This is not to say that I do not stand in awe of the developing embryo, a creation of majestic beauty and mystery. But I stand in equal awe of the Grand Canyon, the spider's web, and quantum mechanics. Awe commands wonder, humility, appreciation. It does not command inviolability. I am quite prepared to shatter an

Cloning for Research Is Impermissible

"Research cloning is more morally objectionable than reproductive cloning in this way: The procedure for research cloning is the same as it is for reproductive cloning until the embryo is implanted. However, engaging in research cloning entails the destruction of an embryo, so therapeutic cloning is ethically wrong, no matter how appealing the consequence of having compatible tissue is or might be to someone. Therefore, research cloning is morally impermissible."

Dave Yount, February 25, 2004.
www.mc.maricopa.edu/~yount/text/dy-anti-cloning-args.pdf.

atom, take down a spider's web, or dam a canyon for electricity. (Though we'd have to be very short on electricity before I'd dam the Grand.)

I do not believe the embryo is entitled to inviolability. But is it entitled to nothing? There is a great distance between inviolability, on the one hand, and mere "thingness," on the other. Many advocates of research cloning see nothing but thingness. That view justifies the most ruthless exploitation of the embryo. That view is dangerous.

Why? Three possible reasons. First, the Brave New World Factor: Research cloning gives man too much power for evil. Second, the Slippery Slope: The habit of embryonic violation is in and of itself dangerous. Violate the blastocyst today and every day, and the practice will inure you to violating the fetus or even the infant tomorrow. Third, Manufacture: The very act of creating embryos for the sole purpose of exploiting and then destroying them will ultimately predispose us to a ruthless utilitarianism about human life itself.

The Brave New World Factor

The physicists at Los Alamos did not hesitate to penetrate, manipulate, and split uranium atoms on the grounds that uranium atoms possess intrinsic worth that entitled them to inviolability. Yet after the war, many fought to curtail atomic power. They feared the consequences of delivering such unfathomable power—and potential evil—into the hands of fallible human beings. Analogously, one could believe that the cloned blastocyst has little more intrinsic worth than the uranium atom and still be deeply troubled by the manipulation of the blastocyst because of the fearsome power it confers upon humankind.

The issue is leverage. Our knowledge of how to manipulate human genetics (or atomic nuclei) is still primitive. We could never construct *ex nihilo* [from nothing] a human embryo. It is an unfolding organism of unimaginable complexity that took nature three billion years to produce. It might take us less time to build it from scratch, but not much less. By that time, we as a species might have acquired enough wisdom to use it wisely. Instead, the human race in its infancy has stumbled upon a genie infinitely too complicated to create or even fully understand, but understandable enough to command and perhaps even control. And given our demonstrated unwisdom with our other great discovery—atomic power: As we speak, the very worst of humanity is on the threshold of acquiring the most powerful weapons in history—this is a fear and a consideration to be taken very seriously.

For example. Female human eggs seriously limit the mass production of cloned embryos. Extracting eggs from women is difficult, expensive, and potentially dangerous. The search is on, therefore, for a good alternative. Scientists have begun injecting human nuclei into the egg cells of animals. In 1996 Massachusetts scientists injected a human nucleus [into] a cow egg. Chinese scientists have fused a human fibroblast with a rabbit egg and have grown the resulting embryo to the blastocyst stage. We have no idea what grotesque results might come from such interspecies clonal experiments.

In October 2000 the first primate containing genes from another species was born (a monkey with a jellyfish gene). In 1995 researchers in Texas produced headless mice. In 1997 researchers in Britain produced headless tadpoles. In theory, headlessness might be useful for organ transplantation. One can envision, in a world in which embryos are routinely manufactured, the production of headless clones—subhuman creatures with usable human organs but no head, no brain, no consciousness to identify them with the human family.

The heart of the problem is this: Nature, through endless evolution, has produced cells with totipotent power. We are about to harness that power for crude human purposes. That should give us pause. Just around the corner lies the logical by-product of such power: human-animal hybrids, partly developed human bodies for use as parts, and other horrors imagined—[Brave New World author Aldous] Huxley's Deltas and Epsilons—and as yet unimagined. This is the Brave New World Factor. Its grounds for objecting to this research are not about the beginnings of life, but about the ends; not the origin of these cells, but their destiny; not where we took these magnificent cells from, but where they are taking us.

"Human cloning ... might turn out to be less frightening than we currently imagine. Market forces might make reproductive cloning impractical, and scientific advancement might make it unnecessary."

Research Cloning Is Not Likely to Be a Threat

Robin Marantz Henig

The fears about human cloning are probably overblown, says science author Robin Marantz Henig. When the first successful in vitro fertilization (IVF) led to the birth of an English girl named Louise Brown in the 1970s, she notes, some said that it would be the end of humanity as we know it. Such claims now seem absurd, Henig argues, but virtually identical charges are being hurled at human cloning. In reality, Henig points out, the failure to fund research into IVF led to its development by market forces alone, with the result that some long-term risks went overlooked. With cloning, Henig suggests, the extreme threats that opponents conjure are unlikely to materialize. Research cloning might actually develop technologies that take away the incentive for repro-

Robin Marantz Henig, "Pandora's Baby," *Scientific American*, vol. 288, June 1, 2003, p. 63. Copyright © 2003 by Scientific American, Inc. All rights reserved. Reprinted with permission. www.sciam.com.

ductive cloning, she contends, by leading to improvements in as-sisted reproduction for infertile men or women. Robin Marantz Henig is a science writer with numerous books to her credit, in-cluding Pandora's Baby, *about the early days of in vitro fertili-zation.*

As you read, consider the following questions:

1. What did early opponents of IVF commonly fear would be lost if the technology was allowed to proceed, accord-ing to Henig?
2. In Henig's opinion, why did antiabortionists object to IVF?
3. What does Henig suggest might be the most common use of reproductive cloning in the future?

On July 25, [2003,] a once-unique person will turn 25. This nursery school aide in the west of England seems like an average young woman, a quiet, shy blonde who enjoys an occasional round of darts at the neighborhood pub. But Louise Brown's birth was greeted by newspaper headlines call-ing her the "baby of the century." Brown was the world's first test-tube baby.

Today people may remember Brown's name, or that she was British, or that her doctors, Steptoe and Edwards, sounded vaguely like a vaudeville act. But the past quarter of a century has dimmed the memory of one of the most important as-pects of her arrival: many people were horrified by it. Even some scientists feared that Patrick Steptoe and Robert Ed-wards might have brewed pestilence in a petri dish. Would the child be normal, or would the laboratory manipulations leave dreadful genetic derangements? Would she be psychologically scarred by the knowledge of how bizarrely she had been cre-ated? And was she a harbinger of a race of unnatural beings who might eventually be fashioned specifically as a means to nefarious ends?

Now that in-vitro fertilization (IVF) has led to the birth of an estimated one million babies worldwide, these fears and speculations may seem quaint and even absurd. But the same concerns once raised about IVF are being voiced, sometimes almost verbatim, about human cloning. Will cloning go the way of IVF, morphing from the monstrous to the mundane? And if human cloning, as well as other genetic interventions on the embryo, does someday become as commonplace as test-tube baby-making, is that to be feared—or embraced? The lessons that have been learned from the IVF experience can illuminate the next decisions to be made.

Then and Now

As IVF moved from the hypothetical to the actual, some considered it to be nothing more than scientists showing off: "The development of test tube babies," one critic remarked, "can be compared to the perfecting of wing transplants so that pigs might fly." But others thought of IVF as a perilous insult to nature. The British magazine *Nova* ran a cover story in the spring of 1972 suggesting that test-tube babies were "the biggest threat since the atom bomb" and demanding that the public rein in the unpredictable scientists. "If today we do not accept the responsibility for directing the biologist," the *Nova* editors wrote, "tomorrow we may pay a bitter price—the loss of free choice and, with it, our humanity. We don't have much time left."

A prominent early enemy of IVF was Leon Kass, a biologist at the University of Chicago who took a professional interest in the emerging field of bioethics. If society allowed IVF to proceed, he wrote shortly after Louise Brown's birth, some enormous issues were at stake: "the idea of the humanness of our human life and the meaning of our embodiment, our sexual being, and our relation to ancestors and descendants."

Now read Kass, a leading detractor of every new form of reproductive technology for the past 30 years, in 2003: "[Cloning] threatens the dignity of human procreation, giving one generation unprecedented genetic control over the next," he wrote in the *New York Times.* "It is the first step toward a eugenic world in which children become objects of manipulation and products of will." Such commentary coming from Kass is particularly noteworthy because of his unique position: . . . he has been the head of President George W. Bush's Council on Bioethics, whose first task was to offer advice on how to regulate human cloning.

Of course, IVF did not wind up creating legions of less than human children, nor did it play a role in the disintegration of the nuclear family, consequences that people like Kass feared. And so many newer, more advanced methods of assisted reproduction have been introduced in the past decade that the "basic IVF" that produced Louise Brown now seems positively routine. One early prediction, however, did turn out to contain more than one kernel of truth. In the 1970s critics cautioned that IVF would set us tumbling down the proverbial slippery slope toward more sophisticated and, to some, objectionable forms of reproductive technology—and that once we opened the floodgates by allowing human eggs to be fertilized in the laboratory, there would be no stopping our descent.

If you consider all the technique that might soon be available to manipulate a developing embryo, it could appear that the IVF naysayers were correct in their assessment of the slipperiness of the slope. After all, none of the genetic interventions now being debated—prenatal genetic diagnosis, gene insertions in sex cells or embryos to correct disease, the creation of new embryonic stem cell lines and, the elephant in the living room, cloning—would even be potentialities had scientists not first learned how to fertilize human eggs in a laboratory dish.

But does the existence of such a slippery slope mean that present reproductive technology research will lead inevitably to developments that some find odious, such as embryos for tissue harvesting, or the even more abhorrent manufacture of human-nonhuman hybrids and human clones? Many people clearly fear so, which explains the current U.S. efforts to curtail scientists' ability to manipulate embryos even before the work gets under way. But those efforts raise the question of whether science that has profound moral and ethical implications should simply never be done. Or should such science proceed, with careful attention paid to the early evolution of certain areas of research so that society can make informed decisions about whether regulation is needed?

IVF Unbound

The frenzy to try to regulate or even outlaw cloning is in part a deliberate attempt not to let it go the way of IVF, which has been a hodgepodge of unregulated activities with no governmental or ethical oversight and no scientific coordination. Ironically, the reason IVF became so ubiquitous and uncontrolled in the U.S. was that its opponents, particularly anti-abortion activists, were trying to stop it completely. Antiabortion activists' primary objection to IVF was that it involved the creation of extra embryos that would ultimately be unceremoniously destroyed—a genocide worse than at any abortion clinic, they believed. Accordingly, they thought that their best strategy would be to keep the federal government from financing IVF research.

A succession of presidential commissions starting in 1973 debated the ethics of IVF but failed to clarify matters. Some of the commissions got so bogged down in abortion politics that they never managed to hold a single meeting. Others concluded that IVF research was ethically acceptable as long as scientists honored the embryo's unique status as a "potential human life," a statement rather than a practical guideline. In 1974 the government banned federal funding for fetal research. It also forbade funding for research on the human em-

bryo (defined as a fetus less than eight weeks old), which includes IVF. In 1993 President Bill Clinton signed the NIH [National Institutes of Health] Revitalization Act, which allowed federal funding of IVF research. (In 1996, however, Congress again banned embryo research.) The bottom line is that despite a series of recommendations from federal bioethics panels stating that taxpayer support of IVF research would be acceptable with certain safeguards in place, the government has never sponsored a single research grant for human IVF.

This lack of government involvement—which would also have served to direct the course of IVF research—led to a funding vacuum, into which rushed entrepreneurial scientists supported by private money. These free agents did essentially whatever they wanted and whatever the market would bear, turning IVF into a cowboy science driven by the marketplace and undertaken without guidance. The profession attempted to regulate itself—in 1986, for example, the American Fertility Society issued ethical and clinical guidelines for its members—but voluntary oversight was only sporadically effective. The quality of clinics, of which there were more than 160 by 1990, remained spotty, and those seeking IVF had little in the way of objective information to help them choose the best ones.

Today, in what appears to be an effort to avoid the mistakes made with IVF, the federal government is actively involved in regulating cloning. With the announcement in 1997 of the birth of Dolly, the first mammal cloned from an adult cell, President Clinton established mechanisms, which remain in place, to prohibit such activities in humans. Congress has made several attempts to outlaw human cloning, most recently with a bill that would make any form of human cloning punishable by a $1-million fine and up to 10 years in prison. (The House of Representatives passed this bill this past winter [2003], but the Senate has yet to debate it.) Politicians thus lumped together two types of cloning that scientists have tried to keep separate: "therapeutic," or "research," cloning, designed to produce embryonic stem cells that might eventually mature into specialized human tissues to treat degenerative diseases; and "reproductive" cloning, undertaken specifically to bring forth a cloned human being. A second bill now before the Senate would explicitly protect research cloning while making reproductive cloning a federal offense.

IVF Risks Revealed

One result of the unregulated nature of IVF is that it took nearly 25 years to recognize that IVF children are at increased medical risk. For most of the 1980s and 1990s, IVF was thought to have no effect on birth outcomes, with the exception of problems associated with multiple births: one third of all IVF pregnancies resulted in twins or triplets, the unintended consequence of the widespread practice of implanting six or eight or even 10 embryos into the womb during each IVF cycle, in the hope that at least one of them would "take." (This bruteforce method also leads to the occasional set of quadruplets.) When early studies raised concerns about the safety of IVF—showing a doubling of the miscarriage rate, a tripling of the rate of stillbirths and neonatal deaths, and a fivefold increase in ectopic pregnancies—many people attributed the problems not to IVF itself but to its association with multiple pregnancies.

By [2002], however, IVF's medical dark side became undeniable. In March 2002 the *New England Journal of Medicine* published two studies that controlled for the increased rate of multiple births among IVF babies and still found problems. One study compared the birth weights of more than 42,000 babies conceived through assisted reproductive technology, including IVF, in the U.S. in 1996 and 1997 with the weights of more than three million babies conceived naturally. Excluding both premature births and multiple births, the test tube babies were still two and a half times as likely to have low birth weights, defined as less than 2,500 grams, or about five and a half pounds. The other study looked at more than 5,000 babies born in Australia between 1993 and 1997, including 22 percent born as a result of IVF. It found that IVF babies were twice as likely as naturally conceived infants to have multiple major birth defects, in particular, chromosomal and musculoskeletal abnormalities. The Australian researchers speculate that these problems may be a consequence of the drugs used to induce ovulation or to maintain pregnancy in its early stages. In addition, factors contributing to infertility may increase the risk of birth defects. The technique of IVF itself also might be to blame. A flawed sperm injected into an egg, as it is in one IVF variation, may have been unable to penetrate the egg on its own and is thus given a chance it would otherwise not have to produce a baby with a developmental abnormality.

Clearly, these risks could remain hidden during more than two decades of experience with IVF only because no system was ever put in place to track results. "If the government had supported IVF, the field would have made much more rapid progress," says Duane Alexander, director of the National Institute of Child Health and Human Development. "But as it is, the institute has never funded human IVF research of any form"—a record that Alexander calls both incredible and embarrassing.

Although the medical downsides of IVF are finally coming to light, many of the more alarmist predictions about where IVF would lead never came to pass. For example, one scenario was that it would bring us "wombs for hire," an oppressed underclass of women paid to bear the children of the infertile rich. But surrogate motherhood turned out to be expensive and emotionally complex for all parties, and it never became widespread.

Human cloning, too, might turn out to be less frightening than we currently imagine. Market forces might make reproductive cloning impractical, and scientific advancement might make it unnecessary. For example, people unable to produce eggs or sperm might ponder cloning to produce offspring. But the technology developed for cloning could make it possible to create artificial eggs or sperm containing the woman's or man's own DNA, which could then be combined with the sperm or egg of a partner. In the future, "cloning" might refer only to what is now being called therapeutic cloning, and it might eventually be truly therapeutic: a laboratory technique for making cells for the regeneration of damaged organs, for example. And some observers believe that the most common use of cloning technology will ultimately not involve human cells at all: the creature most likely to be cloned may wind up being a favorite family dog or cat.

The history of IVF reveals the pitfalls facing cloning if decision making is simply avoided. But despite similarities in societal reactions to IVF and cloning, the two technologies are philosophically quite different. The goal of IVF is to enable sexual reproduction in order to produce a genetically unique human being. Only the site of conception changes, after which events proceed much the way they normally do. Cloning disregards sexual reproduction, its goal being to mimic not the process but the already existing living entity. Perhaps the biggest difference between IVF and cloning, however, is the focus of our anxieties. In the 1970s the greatest fear related to in vitro fertilization was that it would fail, leading to sorrow, disappointment and possibly the birth of grotesquely abnormal babies. Today the greatest fear about human cloning is that it may succeed.

VIEWPOINT 3

> "Will the 'designer children' all end up
> looking and acting the same? Probably
> not."

Parents Should Be Free to Use "Designer Baby" Technologies

Krista Conger

In the following selection Krista Conger argues that fears about genetic enhancements of children are largely misplaced. Parents already make many decisions about their children's futures, and should be allowed to decide whether or not to make use of so-called designer baby technologies as they become available. Although some highly beneficial genetic enhancements might become universal, since tastes and interests differ, the result will not be a generation of identical children, she argues. Rather than attempt to shut off parental choice, the best course, Conger asserts, is to assure equitable access to new technologies. Krista Conger is a science writer on the staff of the Stanford School of Medicine's Office of Communication and Public Affairs.

As you read, consider the following questions:

1. Why does globalization offset some of the fears of a division in the human species, according to Conger?

Krista Conger, "As Good As It Gets?" *Stanford Medicine Magazine*, summer 2006. Reproduced by permission.

2. What does the author give as an example of a genetic enhancement that might become universal?

3. What does sex selection in the United States indicate about "designer baby" technologies, according to Conger?

In October of 1925, the Rollins family traveled nearly 300 miles from San Antonio to Dallas to enter the Texas State Fair's second annual Fitter Families Contest. Competition was fierce: More than 50 families flocked to a building next to the cattle pens to be judged on their physical, mental and moral qualifications. Comparisons with livestock breeding were unavoidable and intentional. They were also met with unbridled enthusiasm.

"I consider the Fitter Family Exhibit at the fair the most important feature of this year's exposition," family patriarch O. B. Rollins, an agricultural agent, told the *Dallas Morning News* at that time. "For years I have been interested in better livestock in our state and in the betterment of plants. And now I am interested in the betterment of the men and women of the state." Rollins no doubt found his vote of confidence and the long trip worthwhile when his family of seven took top honors in the competition.

The contests, which were held at various state fairs nationwide in the early '20s, were a bid by the fledgling American Eugenics Society to encourage those marriages they considered most likely to generate physically and mentally fit children. For a time, members of the society even toyed with the idea of "certifying" families and encouraging marriage only between people of equal status. Like modern-day [Gregor] Mendels, they thought that careful breeding of select individuals, coupled with forced sterilization of the feeble-minded and shiftless, would eventually yield a superior class of Americans capable of advancing both the country and the human race.

Such hubris seems both laughable and alarming now. Studies of human genetics and evolution have taught us that many favorable qualities—intelligence, physical fitness and mental health, for example—are outward manifestations of complex interactions between many genes and their environment. Even without the very real ethical concerns that go hand-in-hand with the value judgments implicit in such a program, simply landing an attractive, healthy mate doesn't guarantee superior offspring.

A Complex Genetic Tapestry

Why bother to try to improve ourselves, anyway? Aren't we already at the top of our game? After all, like other species, modern humans have been evolving for hundreds of thousands of years in an intricate dance of adaptation and selection. The complexity of some of the steps is breathtaking. Sickle cell anemia has been endemic in African populations for about 3,000 years because the genetic culprit, when present in just one copy, also confers protection against an even more deadly regional foe: malaria.

It's difficult to imagine that we could have choreographed such a delicate trade-off. Maybe we should leave well enough alone and let the natural forces continue to pound away at us like an enthusiastic physical trainer.

On the other hand, we're now more able than ever to isolate ourselves from the selective forces that got us this far. We cure ourselves of formerly fatal diseases, we twist the thermostat dials in our houses up and down according to our whims, and, instead of running from predators on the savannah, we watch them on cable. From this perspective, it seems that the evolutionary tango as we know it has stopped. No wonder the Rollins family cast their lot with those who felt our species' future was better off in human hands.

Maybe they were right. Recent advances in medical technology have made attainable many things that our grandparents would have thought impossible. Sperm banks provide a wide array of choices for women who favor nature over nurture, prenatal testing for disease is commonplace, and couples undergoing in-vitro fertilization can be choosy as to which of several embryos they implant. If these changes seem revolutionary, however, we should brace ourselves for the biggest upset of all: our coming ability to modify our own and our children's genomes in ways that will persist for generations. . . .

Cultural Intervention

"This is not the first time humans have directed their own evolution," says evolutionary biologist Marcus Feldman, PhD, the Burnet C. and Mildred Finley Wohlford Professor in Stanford's School of Humanities and Sciences. "Inventions of agriculture and cities caused new food allergies and infections, respectively, which had biological reactions whose strength depended on genes. Our cultural evolution overtook human biological evolution thousands of years ago." In other words, truly natural selective forces were supplanted by those of our own making long ago. . . .

Although there's no way of knowing exactly what biological and technological advances will be available in the coming decades, there are some obvious candidates that have already proven their mettle in yeast or mammals. Introducing genetic modifications into the egg and sperm, for example, called germline modification, ensures that every cell of the subsequent fetus will carry the newly introduced change, as will every one of that child's progeny. Alternatively, an artificial chromosome or two could carry a payload of advantageous genes into future generations. Applied across the board, modifications that increase life span or physical endurance could theoretically impact human evolution in ways that make mere city building seem puny. . . .

Limited Impact

However, these types of technologies aren't likely to affect the course of human evolution unless they become available to many more people. Only about one in every 100 children in

Designer Babies Will Find Acceptance

"Pre-implantation genetic diagnosis, which is embryo screening, already exists. It's been done for about 10 years. The avoidance of disease through these technologies is going to become increasingly commonplace, as in-vitro fertilization becomes easier, and as the range of genetic testing is increased. The challenging part of that is going to be when tests are done for things that are not strictly disease related, like personality and temperament. . . . I think that future humans are going to look back at this period now, and see it as a very, very primitive time. I think they're going to go: 'My God, people used to live into their 70s, and then they died of horrible diseases at that young age, and children were just the problem of this random meeting of sperm and egg. This is really strange.'"

Gregory Stock, Salon.com, May 25, 2002.

the United States is conceived via in-vitro fertilization, and only a fraction of these undergo disease screening before implantation. Germline modifications are far more technologically challenging. Gregory Stock, director of UCLA's Program on Medicine, Technology and Society, estimates in his 2003 book, *Redesigning Humans*, that germline therapy would have to be used at least 100 times more often than the predicted demand to even begin to make a splash in the human gene pool.

But human society is not one big pool. Cultural differences thwart genetic mixing; they could lead to a genetically stratified society. Those who have access to future germline interventions could use them to give their children every available advantage, cocooning themselves and their descendants in a cozy genetic bubble of their own making. If this separation is maintained over thousands of years, or if one single change gives carriers a unique genetic advantage such as a significantly longer life span, it's possible that we could see a marked separation between population groups.

Most experts think that's unlikely.

"Throughout the history of medicine, effective innovations have typically become widely diffused across income levels," says Victor Fuchs, PhD, Stanford's Henry J. Kaiser Jr. Professor of Economics (Emeritus). "We can see this when we look at patterns of change in mortality and life expectancy in countries like India, where most people can expect to live well into their 60s. For their average income level, we'd expect them to have a life expectancy decades shorter. All of the poorer countries are way above where we would expect them to be if they weren't benefiting from technologies and ideas developed elsewhere. Particularly in the case of genetic modifications, I don't think we're talking about anything that is going to be so clearly effective and yet so expensive that it's only available to certain subsets of the population. That's just not in the cards."

What's more, increasing globalization will lead to more mixing of genes, not less, to the benefit of all.

"Genes that in the past have been physically separated by oceans are still kept apart by cultural and social norms," says [Stanford human evolution expert Peter] Underhill. "As these cultural boundaries become more porous, we set the stage for mixing genes at a higher frequency, which may lead to a phenomenon known as hybrid vigor and make all of our descendents more healthy." Take that, eugenics society!

Variety Will Persist

But what if human society reached the critical mass of genetically altered offspring needed to change evolutionary course? Will the "designer children" all end up looking and acting the same? Probably not. Although some hypothetical attributes, like foolproof protection against cancer, would probably be universally sought by people with the financial means to design their babies, other traits, such as personality types or physical attributes, would depend largely on a prospective parent's personal choice. That we see such individual differences in choices even with today's rudimentary technologies bodes well for our ability to avoid a future filled with über-clones [superbeings], observes Gene Hoyme, MD, a medical geneticist at Lucile Packard Children's Hospital and director of its biochemical genetics laboratory.

For example, even though sex selection of embryos fertilized in vitro has many people up in arms, there's no evidence that it's on track to alter the gender balance in this country: Boys and girls are nearly equally sought after, says Hoyme. And although some parents will terminate a pregnancy if the fetus has a genetic or developmental problem that they feel isn't compatible with a meaningful life, different families draw this line at dramatically different points in the sand. For some, it's too much to consider having a child with Down syndrome. For others it's important to sustain life as long as possible regardless of the severity of the condition. Still others might choose to have a child as similar to them as possible, down to sharing disabilities such as deafness.

Parents Choose Kids' Paths

"Eugenics is here now," says Stanford bioethicist David Magnus, PhD. "So what? We allow parents to have virtually unlimited control over what school their child attends, what church they go to and how much exercise they get. All of these things have a much bigger impact on a child's future than the limited genetic choices available to us now. As long as these are safe and effective, why not give parents this option as well?" A much more pressing problem, according to Magnus, is the varying levels of access to critical health and educational resources experienced by poor and minority populations.

"I just don't see the whole human genome careening off in some dramatic trajectory due to genetic interventions when we can't even get everyone vaccinated," agrees Underhill.

Some experts also warn that parents who choose specific genetic interventions might be disappointed if the child does not live up to their expectations. Prioritizing life goals for an unborn child denies the child his or her "right to an open future," they believe. Magnus disagrees. Parents are just as likely to be disappointed, he says, if they spend time and money on music lessons for a child who turns out to have a tin ear.

"Parents close doors for their children all the time," he says. "That's part of being a parent." Underhill hypothesizes that genetic modifications could one day be viewed as optional enhancements that parents may or may not choose for their children.

As our technological abilities and knowledge of genetics increase, the only thing we can be sure of is that the temptation to control the nature of our children will grow. Ensuring that no one group attempts to mandate the outcome of these decisions and that as many people as possible have access to the technology might help us to walk that delicate line between improving and irreparably dividing the human race. After all, how can we deny Rollins' urge to spend at least as much time thinking about our own future as we do the animals and plants at the fairgrounds?

"The nation is already sliding down a slippery slope toward the age of reprogenetics. Our only hope of slowing the pace is to apply the brakes of regulation."

Society Should Restrict "Designer Baby" Technologies

Shannon Brownlee

In the following selection Shannon Brownlee decries the rise of unregulated reprogenetics—the combination of reproductive technology with genetic manipulation. With federally funded research in this area largely shelved by politics, she warns, the profit motive is driving innovations in reproductive technology. All that prevents "designer babies" from being on the market is the ethics of fertility clinic operators, she says. To head off the problem, Brownlee argues, greater federal regulation is needed. Medical journalist Shannon Brownlee is a senior Markle Fellow at the New America Foundation.

As you read, consider the following questions:

1. What incentives do fertility clinics have to influence pregnancy rates, according to Brownlee?

2. What does the author say the history of medicine reveals about new treatments?

3. How does Brownlee regard England's fertility licensing board?

In the mid-1990s, embryologist Jacques Cohen pioneered a promising new technique for helping infertile women have children. His technique, known as cytoplasmic transfer, was intended to "rescue" the eggs of infertile women who had undergone repeated, unsuccessful attempts at in-vitro fertilization, or IVF. It involved injecting the cytoplasm found inside the eggs of a fertile donor, into the patient's eggs.

When the first baby conceived through cytoplasmic transfer was born in 1997, the press instantly hailed Cohen's technique as yet another technological miracle. But four years later, the real story has proven somewhat more complicated. [In 2001,] Cohen and his colleagues at the Institute for Reproductive Medicine and Science of St. Barnabas, a New Jersey fertility clinic, set off alarm bells among bioethicists with the publication of a paper detailing the genetic condition of two of the 17 cytoplasmic-transfer babies born through the clinic to date. The embryologists reported that they had endowed the children with extra bits of a special type of genetic material, known as mitochondrial DNA, or mtDNA, which came with the cytoplasm transferred from the donor eggs to the patient's.

That meant the resulting children had three genetic parents: mother, father, and mtDNA donor. It also meant that female children would transmit their unorthodox combination of mitochondrial DNA to their own offspring (mtDNA is passed down only through eggs), with unknown implications. In effect, Cohen had created the first bioengineered babies. As Cohen's group noted, their experiment was "The first case of human [inheritable] genetic modification resulting in normal, healthy children."

Signs of Trouble

Just how normal those children will turn out to be is anybody's guess. At a recent meeting in Europe, the New Jersey researchers reported that one of the children conceived through cytoplasmic transfer has been diagnosed with "pervasive developmental disorder," a catch-all term for symptoms that range from mild delays in speech to autism. Cohen's group maintained that it is extremely unlikely that cytoplasmic transfer and the resulting mishmash of mtDNA is to blame.

But geneticists have only begun to trace the connections between mtDNA and a host of diseases ranging from strange metabolic ailments to diabetes and Lou Gehrig's disease, and some experts argued that the child's disorder may well be caused by a mismatch between the donor and mother's mtDNA. As Jim Cummins, a molecular biologist at Murdoch University in Western Australia, put it: "To deliberately create individuals with multiple mitochondrial genotypes without knowing the consequences is really a step into the dark."

Welcome to the murky world of "reprogenetics," as Princeton biologist Lee Silver has dubbed the merger between the science of genetics and the fertility industry. While much of the nation's attention has been focused on human cloning, a possibility that is still largely theoretical, a massive, uncontrolled experiment in bioengineering humans is well underway in the Wild West of American fertility clinics, as Cohen and his colleagues have demonstrated. Indeed, there has been more debate over—and far more research into—the implications of bioengineered corn than of bioengineered humans.

Now, many bioethicists believe that Cohen's experiment with cytoplasmic transfer was just one more small step towards a world in which eugenics is another name for making babies. Today, any couple with several thousand dollars to spare can choose the sex of their offspring, while parents who are carriers for certain genetic disorders can undergo IVF and have the resulting embryos genetically tested to ensure their children are free of disease. Tomorrow, parents may be able to enhance their offspring with designer genes. One day, the fertility industry's efforts to help couples conceive could bring society to the brink of altering the genetic heritage of the species.

All that currently stands in the way of parents bent on practicing homegrown eugenics are the ethics of individual fertility specialists and the technical hurdles. Most fertility doctors have the best of intentions, to help patients get pregnant, and to avoid transmitting debilitating disease. And it is by no means certain that science will ever be able to offer parents the option of bioengineering their offspring.

All the same, the pace of the technology is dizzying. . . .

Driven by Profit

With so much money at stake, the market for fertility services is highly competitive, but without government regulation or oversight, the infertility business has become a bit like the dietary supplement industry. There are lots of miraculous claims but not much data to back them up—and tremendous financial incentive to push the envelope with radical new products.

For instance, not all clinics are equally adept at producing babies. Clinic success rates have improved steadily over the last few years, from an average of 17 percent in 1992 for women under 40, to nearly 30 percent in 1999, the most recent year for which figures are available. But these rates vary wildly, from as low as 14 percent to as high as 60 percent.

And babies, of course, are what patients are paying for—usually out of their own pockets, because most insurers do not cover IVF treatment. Clinics have strong financial incentives to inflate their pregnancy rates, or at least to persuade prospective patients that their chances of getting pregnant are high. The largest clinics have substantial advertising budgets,

Children's Rights Deserve Consideration

"A lot of people would argue that parents' being able to make genetic choices is just an extension of the kind of existing personal autonomy that people enjoy in liberal societies. But I think that there's a real question about the degree to which you can assume the consent of the child that you are creating. The best case of this is this recent one where there was a deaf lesbian couple that chose to implant a deaf embryo, and now they've got two deaf children, because they wanted to preserve this deaf culture within their family. Is that really in the best interests of their child?"

Francis Fukuyama, Salon.com, May 21, 2002.

and they market heavily to primary care physicians, who refer patients to clinics, with lavish dinners and seminars in exotic locales.

The fertility industry's self-promotion has gone largely unchallenged, either by the media or the scientific community. While the press has hailed each new development as a godsend for desperate would-be parents, with headlines such as "Amazing Medical Breakthrough" and "New Hope for Infertile Couples," medical researchers who may doubt the validity of these claims have for the most part remained mute. That's because the ban on federal funding for embryo research has made objective analysis of new techniques nearly impossible, and have left infertile couples the unwitting participants in a vast experiment of largely untested technology.

Scientific development in the field has fallen not to high-caliber, federally funded embryologists, but instead to the clinics themselves, which use profits from patients to conduct research. The technology has proceeded with minimal government oversight and peer review, and in the opinion of many biologists, has suffered in quality as a result. "There is no real hard-core scientific background on the part of many of the individuals who are doing this work," says Jonathan Van Blerkom, a leading embryologist at the University of Colorado. Clinics focus their efforts almost exclusively on increasing pregnancy rates, often with little regard for the basic biology and potential consequences to patients and babies. . . .

Undue Haste

It is also true, however, that the history of medicine is littered with examples of doctors unquestioningly adopting new treatments long before they have been evaluated, only to abandon them when they turn out to be ineffective—or worse. More than 30,000 women with breast cancer received high dose chemotherapy with bone-marrow transplants in the 1980s and 90s. At least 9,000 died from the treatment before researchers finally performed clinical trials, which ultimately demonstrated that high dosage is no better than standard chemotherapy regimens.

The deeper question, of course, is why we allow uncontrolled experimentation on human subjects in any branch of medicine. But the issue is particularly pressing for reproductive technologies, especially now that fertility centers are wading into the uncharted waters of the gene pool. . . .

Under the current political landscape, the nation has little control over what it deems acceptable. Americans may one day decide that it is perfectly all right to genetically engineer children with blue skin or webbed feet or any other trait that parents see fit. In the meantime, current practices in the fertility industry could use some oversight. Thus far, however, the only legislative response to worrisome reproductive technologies has been to ban them and accuse their practitioners of "playing God," an argument that appeals to conservative constituents but will in the short term, at least, prove futile. Says former bioethics committee member [R. Alta] Charo, "As soon as you have absolute prohibitions you run into constitutional challenges."

Role for Regulators

Over the long term, banning certain technologies, such as reproductive cloning, may well be advisable, but reining in the pace of reprogenetics now is going to take a network of regulatory solutions. First on the list: Update the FDA's [food and drug administration] decades-old charter. In recent years, Congress has generally sided with business against the agency, beating back its efforts to rein in the herbal medicine industry, for example. But legislators have already signaled their distaste for reproductive cloning, and the balance of power is likely to shift when it comes to giving the FDA regulatory control over reprogenetics.

The FDA, along with the U.S. Department of Health and Human Services (HHS), jointly oversee the protection of human subjects in clinical trials, which are required to demonstrate safety and efficacy before new drugs or medical devices can be licensed for market. Most of the time, companies put their products through rigorous testing in animals long before proceeding to human experimentation. Applying the same standards to human embryo experiments would compel fertility clinics to perform similar tests before subjecting patients to new reprogenetic technologies. It would also entail the creation of specialized review boards with the expertise to evaluate human reproductive experiments. . . .

England's Example

England also offers a model for creating boundaries for thornier issues bordering on eugenics. A decade after the birth of the first test-tube baby, Parliament created a licensing board, the Human Fertilization and Embryology Authority (HFEA), which has kept a tight lid on burgeoning genetic technologies since 1991—to the dismay of some would-be patients and clinic directors.

In a recent case before the HFEA, for example, a family with four boys that had lost their young daughter in a fire asked to be allowed to choose female embryos for IVF. HFEA refused, fearing that sex selection for purposes other than to prevent a sex-linked disease, such as hemophilia, would push British society toward eugenics, or at least widespread sex-selection. A national licensing board like the HFEA would probably prove unworkable in this country, but the U.S. would do well to create an advisory panel for reproductive technologies that would provide a public forum for what are now individual decisions with huge social consequences.

Finally, anti-abortion activists need to recognize that federal involvement in embryo research is critical for limiting the risks posed by genetic engineering of the future and improving the current outcomes for families desperately seeking to have a child. Tens of thousands of embryos are discarded by fertility clinics each year because embryologists are not allowed to work on them using federal dollars. If conservatives wish to ban the creation of embryos for the purpose of research, they should focus their formidable political power on allowing research on embryos created in the hopes of producing a child.

Funding such science would certainly bring a higher level of rigor to the field and increased oversight of human experimentation. The nation is already sliding down a slippery slope toward the age of reprogenetics. Our only hope of slowing the pace is to apply the brakes of regulation.

Periodical Bibliography

The following articles have been selected to supplement the diverse views presented in this chapter.

Adam Greene
"The World After Dolly: International Regulation of Human Cloning," *George Washington Journal of International Law and Economics*, vol. 33, 2001.

Samuel D. Hensley
"Designer Babies: One Step Closer," Center for Bioethics and Human Dignity, July 1, 2004. www.cbhd.org/resources/reproductive/hensley_2004-07-01.htm.

Constance Holden
"Sperm-Free Fertilization," *Science*, July 20, 2001.

Steve Johnson
"Cloning Prospects Multiplying: Boom in Animal Products Possible from Advances," *San Jose* (CA) *Mercury News*, August 23, 2005. www.mercurynews.com/mld/mercurynews/12452067.htm.

Aniruddha Malpani
"Why Are We Scared Of Cloning?" *Dr. Malpani.com*, accessed November 2006. www.drmalpani.com/cloning.htm.

Hugh McLachlan
"Ignore the Boys from Brazil—Say Yes to Human Cloning," Reproductive Cloning Network, 2005. www.reproductivecloning.net.

Emily Nash
"First UK Designer Baby Joy," *Daily Mirror* (London), August 5, 2005. www.mirror.co.uk/news/tm_objectid=15821231&method=full&siteid=94762&headline=first-uk-designer-baby-joy--name_page.html.

Shaun D. Pattinson
"Reproductive Cloning: Can Cloning Harm the Clone?" *Medical Law Review*, October 2002.

Wesley J. Smith
"Close the Door on Cloning," *National Review Online*, January 14, 2002. www.nationalreview.com/comment/comment.smith011402.shtml.

For Further Discussion

Chapter 1

1. Reproductive technologies help some infertile people to have babies, but they may hurt others—egg donors, for example, or infertile people who spend all their savings but still fail to produce offspring. Does the benefit to some outweigh the harm to others? Explain your answer.

2. Many issues in society break down along established political lines. Abortion is a good example. Liberals generally favor a woman's right to choose; conservatives generally oppose it. As this chapter shows, however, responses to reproductive technologies evoke differing responses across the political spectrum. Liberals disagree with liberals; conservatives differ with conservatives. Why do you think that is? Explain your reasoning.

Chapter 2

1. Many of the opponents of in vitro fertilization have a specific religious belief: that a human individual begins at conception. Not all religions share this view, however. (Scientists agree that a new human genome is created at conception, but point out that later in development twins may form or no fetus may develop at all.) What is the appropriate role for religious beliefs in deciding public policy?

2. In this chapter, John A. Robertson argues for the rights of parents, Ingrid Schneider argues for the rights of individuals, and Rogeer Hoedemaekers argues for the rights of embryos. If all these rights are in conflict, whose rights should prevail over the others? Explain your reasoning.

3. At the heart of ethical controversies over reproductive

technologies is the embryo. Rogeer Hoedemaekers says they should have the same rights as babies; Michael J. Sandel says they should not. Whose arguments do you find more convincing? Why?

Chapter 3

1. Sex selection is increasingly possible prior to conception. In such a case, the parents are happy, the child is loved, and no one is harmed. Or are they? Explain your stand.

2. In vitro fertilization produces a lot of extra embryos. Some people want these extra embryos to be put up for adoption. Daniel I. Wallance thinks that that is a good idea, but Arthur Caplan argues that it is not. Where do you come down on this issue and why?

3. Reproductive technologies make it possible for a woman of almost any age to become a mother. Should government set a limit on the age of a woman seeking to get pregnant through technology? Cite from the viewpoints in your answer.

Chapter 4

1. Cloning of mammals has already been achieved, but no case of a baby born from human cloning has been proven. Should research in this area be allowed to continue? Why or why not?

2. Advance reproductive technology can help parents to avoid passing genetic diseases on to their children; however, the same technology could make "designer babies" possible. Should parents be allowed to choose characteristics of their babies? Explain your answer.

3. Many scientists want to pursue what they call therapeutic cloning. It involves the creation of an embryo, but the embryo is never implanted so it does not become a baby. Robin Marantz Henig argues that this research is valu-

able—it may lead to new cures—and harmless. Charles Krauthammer argues that it will cause harm and should be banned. Whose arguments do you find more persuasive? Why?

Organizations to Contact

The editors have compiled the following list of organizations concerned with the issues debated in this book. The descriptions are derived from materials provided by the organizations. All have publications or information available for interested readers. The list was compiled on the date of publication of the present volume; the information provided here may change. Be aware that many organizations take several weeks or longer to respond to inquiries, so allow as much time as possible.

American Fertility Association (AFA)
305 Madison Ave., Suite 449, New York, NY   10165
(888) 917-3777 • fax: (718) 601-7722
e-mail: info@theafa.org
Web site: www.theafa.org

A nonprofit organization that educates the public about fertility issues, the AFA also advocates for support for infertile people and access to reproductive technologies. Newsletters and a resource directory are available at its Web site, but users must first complete a free registration form.

American Society for Reproductive Medicine (ASRM)
1209 Montgomery Hwy., Birmingham, AL   35216-2809
(205) 978-5000 • fax: (205) 978-5005
Web site: www.asrm.org

ASRM is an organization that represents practitioners in the field of reproductive technology and medicine. It advocates for the advancement of the art, science, and practice of reproductive medicine. Its Web site includes publicly available fact sheets, booklets, and news, as well as a private section for members only.

Association of Reproductive Health Professionals (ARHP)
2401 Pennsylvania Ave. NW, Suite 350

Washington, DC   20037
(202) 466-3825 • fax: (202) 466-3826

The Association of Reproductive Health Professionals is a nonprofit membership association composed of experts in reproductive health. Its members include physicians, nurse practitioners, nurse midwives, physician assistants, and other professionals in reproductive health. The ARHP's Web site offers brochures and fact sheets in English and Spanish.

Center for Bioethics and Human Dignity
2065 Half Day Rd., Bannockburn, IL   60015
(847) 317-8180 • fax: (847) 317-8101
e-mail: info@cbhd.org
Web site: www.cbhd.org

The Center for Bioethics and Human Dignity explores the potential contribution of biblical values to analysis of bioethical issues. It generally promotes a negative response to reproductive technologies, especially those that involve destruction of embryos. Its Web site offers numerous articles on topics that include designer babies, human cloning, and reproductive ethics.

Center for Genetics and Society
436 Fourteenth St., Suite 700, Oakland, CA   94612
(510) 625-0819 • fax (510) 625-0874
Web site: www.genetics-and-society.org

The Center for Genetics and Society is a nonprofit information and public affairs organization working to encourage responsible uses and effective societal governance of the new human genetic and reproductive technologies. It takes the view that while some reproductive technologies are beneficial, others are harmful and should be banned. The site has a number of position papers available for review.

Centers for Disease Control and Prevention (CDC)
1600 Clifton Rd., Atlanta, GA   30333

(404) 639-3534
Web site: www.cdc.gov/reproductivehealth/ART/

The CDC is the federal government's main public health agency. Its Web site hosts a wealth of information and its assisted reproductive technology (ART) page contains an extensive collection of reports and consumer advice.

Food and Drug Administration (FDA)
5600 Fishers Lane, Rockville, MD   20857
(888) 463-6332)
Web site: www.fda.gov

The FDA is the federal regulatory agency with primary jurisdiction over in vitro fertilization and cloning technologies. Its Web site contains numerous consumer articles, warning letters, and information on these issues.

Human Genome Project
1060 Commerce Park, MS 6480, Oak Ridge, TN   37830
(865) 576-6669 • fax: (865) 574-9888
genome@science.doe.gov
Web site: www.ornl.gov/sci/techresources/Human_Genome/home.shtml

The U.S. Department of Energy oversees the federal government's Human Genome Project. In collaboration with private-sector partners, it deciphered the human genome in 2003 and continues research into human genetic variation. Its Web site includes extensive FAQ information on human cloning and genetic issues.

International Council on Infertility
Information Dissemination (INCIID)
PO Box 6836, Arlington, VA   22206
(703) 379-9178 • fax: (703) 379-1593
Web site: www.inciid.org

INCIID is a nonprofit organization dedicated to the exchange of information between fertility experts and those who suffer from infertility. Its Web site includes forums for members and information on the group's programs.

IVF Connections
www.ivfconnections.com

This virtual organization is a user-run forum and information site for consumers interested in in vitro fertilization.

National Conference of State Legislatures
444 North Capitol St. NW, Suite 515, Washington, DC 20001
(202) 624-5400 • fax: (202) 737-1069
Web site: www.ncsl.org/programs/health/genetics/art.htm

The National Conference of State Legislatures is a bipartisan organization that serves the legislators and staffs of America's fifty states, commonwealths, and territories. Its Web site includes a useful survey of state laws on assisted reproduction as well as background information on related issues.

Organization of Parents Through Surrogacy (OPTS)
PO Box 611, Gurnee, IL 60031
(847) 782-0224
Web site: www.opts.com

OPTS is a not-for-profit, all-volunteer educational, networking, and referral organization that supports infertile couples to build families through surrogate parenting and other assisted reproductive technologies. Its Web site includes surrogacy information resources, legislative alerts, and user forums.

RESOLVE: The National Infertility Association
7910 Woodmont Ave., Suite 1350, Bethesda, MD 20814
(301) 652-8585 • fax: (301) 652-9375
Web site: www.resolve.org

RESOLVE is a nonprofit organization whose chapters are dedicated to the promotion of access to all reproductive options for people experiencing infertility or other reproductive disorders. It advocates on behalf of the reproductive technology industry and fertility patients before the public and policy makers. Its Web site includes information, and the organization also produces printed fact sheets.

Bibliography of Books

Robin Baker   *Sex in the Future: The Reproductive*
                       Revolution and How It Will Change
                       Us. New York: Arcade, 2000.

Christopher L.R.   *Male Fertility and Infertility.* Cam-
Barratt and   bridge, England: Cambridge Univer-
Timothy D.   sity Press, 1999.
Glover

Gay Becker   *The Elusive Embryo: How Women and*
                       Men Approach New Reproductive
                       Technologies. Berkeley and Los Ange-
                       les: University of California Press,
                       2000.

Iwo Brosens   *The Challenge of Reproductive Medi-*
                       cine at Catholic Universities: Time to
                       Leave the Catacombs. Leuven, Bel-
                       gium: Peeters, 2006.

Joan C. Callahan,   *Reproduction, Ethics and the Law:*
ed.   *Feminist Perspectives.* Bloomington:
                       Indiana University Press, 2004.

Susan Cooper   *Choosing Assisted Reproduction: So-*
and Ellen Glazer   *cial, Emotional and Ethical Consider-*
                       ations. Indianapolis: Perspectives,
                       1998.

Dena S. Davis   *Genetic Dilemmas: Reproductive Tech-*
                       nology, Parental Choices, and
                       Children's Futures. New York: Rout-
                       ledge, 2001.

Tommaso Falcone   *Overcoming Infertility.* Cleveland,
                       OH: Cleveland Clinic Press, 2006.

Elizabeth Swire   *The Infertility Survival Handbook.*
Falker   New York: Penguin, 2004.

Sarah Franklin   *Born and Made: An Ethnography of*
and Celia Roberts   *Preimplantation Genetic Diagnosis.*
                      Princeton, NJ: Princeton University
                      Press, 2006.

Roger Gosden   *Designing Babies: The Brave New*
                      World of Reproductive Technology.
                      New York: W.H. Freeman, 1999.

Donna J. Haraway   *Simians, Cyborgs, and Women: The*
                      Reinvention of Nature. New York:
                      Routledge, 1991.

John Harris and   *The Future of Human Reproduction:*
Soren Holm, eds.   *Ethics, Choice, and Regulation.* New
                      York: Oxford University Press, 2000.

Edwin C. Hui   *At the Beginning of Life: Dilemmas in*
                      Theological Bioethics. Downers Grove,
                      IL: InterVarsity, 2002.

Richard T. Hull,   *Ethical Issues in the New Reproductive*
ed.   *Technologies.* Amherst, NY:
                      Prometheus, 2005.

Marcia C. Inhorn   *Infertility Around the Globe: New*
and Frank van   *Thinking on Childlessness, Gender,*
Balen, eds.   *and Reproductive Technologies.* Berke-
                      ley and Los Angeles: University of
                      California Press, 2002.

Leon R. Kass, ed.   *Human Cloning and Human Dignity:*
                      An Ethical Inquiry. Collingdale, PA:
                      Diane Publishing, 2002.

Kerry Lynn Macintosh   *Illegal Beings: Humans Clones and the Law.* New York: Cambridge University Press, 2005.

Alexina McWhinnie   *Families Following Assisted Conception: What Do We Tell Our Child?* Dundee, Scotland: University of Dundee, 1996.

Rozanne Nathalie   *Our Beautiful Work of A.R.T.* Minneapolis, MN: Beaver's Pond, 2002.

Philip G. Peters Jr.   *How Safe Is Safe Enough? Obligations to the Children of Reproductive Technology.* New York: Oxford University Press, 2003.

Karen Peterson-Iyer   *Designer Children: Reconciling Genetic Technology, Feminism, and Christian Faith.* Cleveland, OH: Pilgrim, 2004.

Marlo M. Schalesky   *Empty Womb, Aching Heart: Hope and Help for Those Struggling with Infertility.* Minneapoli, MNs: Bethany House, 2001.

Staff of RESOLVE, with Diane Aronson   *Resolving Infertility: Understanding the Options and Choosing Solutions When You Want to Have a Baby.* New York: Collins & Brown, 2001.

Judith S. Turiel   *Beyond Second Opinions: Rethinking Questions About Fertility.* Berkeley and Los Angeles: University of California Press, 1998.

U.S. Senate Committee on the Judiciary — *Human Cloning: Must We Sacrifice Medical Research in the Name of a Total Ban?* Honolulu: University Press of the Pacific, 2005.

Carol Frost Vercollone, Heidi Moss, and Robert Moss — *Helping the Stork: The Choices and Challenges of Donor Insemination.* New York: John Wiley & Sons, 1997.

Mary Warnock — *Making Babies: Is There a Right to Have Children?* New York: Oxford University Press, 2003.

Index